Sermons For Pentecost II Based On Gospel Texts For Cycle C

All Stirred Up

Richard W. Patt

CSS Publishing Company, Inc., Lima, Ohio

SERMONS FOR PENTECOST II BASED ON GOSPEL TEXTS FOR CYCLE C:
ALL STIRRED UP

Copyright © 1997 by
CSS Publishing Company, Inc.
Lima, Ohio

All rights reserved. No part of this publication may be reproduced in any manner whatsoever without the prior permission of the publisher, except in the case of brief quotations embodied in critical articles and reviews. Inquiries should be addressed to: Permissions, CSS Publishing Company, Inc., P.O. Box 4503, Lima, Ohio 45802-4503.

Scripture quotations are from the *Revised Standard Version of the Bible,* copyrighted 1946, 1952 ©, 1973, by the Division of Christian Education of the National Council of the Churches of Christ in the USA. Used by permission.

Library of Congress Cataloging-in-Publication Data

Patt, Richard W.
    Sermons for Pentecost II based on Gospel texts for cycle C : all stirred up / Richard W. Patt.
      p.   cm.
    ISBN 0-7880-1040-9 (pbk.)
    1. Pentecost season—Sermons.   2. Bible, N.T. Gospels—Sermons.   3. Sermons, American.   I. Title
BV4300.5.P38   1997
252'.64—dc21   96-53192
                                                                                                           CIP

This book is available in the following formats, listed by ISBN:
    0-7880-1040-9   Book

PRINTED IN U.S.A.

To all those (thousands!) who, whenever they discovered that I am a sinner, kept eye contact, validating the Gospel they claimed for themselves.

Editor's Note Regarding The Lectionary

During the past two decades there has been an attempt to move in the direction of a uniform lectionary among various Protestant denominations.

Preaching on the same scripture lessons every Sunday is a step in the right direction of uniting Christians of many faiths. If we are reading the same scriptures together, we may also begin to accomplish other achievements. Our efforts will be strengthened through our unity.

Beginning with Advent 1995 The Evangelical Lutheran Church in America dropped its own lectionary schedule and adopted the Revised Common Lectionary.

Reflecting this change, resources published by CSS Publishing Company put their major emphasis on the Revised Common Lectionary texts for the church year.

Table Of Contents

Foreword	7
Preface	9

Proper 11
Pentecost 9
Ordinary Time 16
    All Stirred Up
    Luke 10:38-42
	11

Proper 12
Pentecost 10
Ordinary Time 17
    It's Okay To Stir Up God
    Luke 11:1-13
	19

Proper 13
Pentecost 11
Ordinary Time 18
    Rich In God's Sight
    Luke 12:13-21
	27

Proper 14
Pentecost 12
Ordinary Time 19
    The Fear Of Taking The Plunge
    Luke 12:32-40
	33

Proper 15
Pentecost 13
Ordinary Time 20
    Peace And The Peacemakers
    Luke 12:49-56
	41

Proper 16   47
(Pentecost 14)
Ordinary Time 21
    Sabotaging The Sabbath
    Luke 13:10-17

Proper 17   53
Pentecost 15
Ordinary Time 22
    A Ministry Of Hospitality
    Luke 14:1, 7-14

Proper 18   59
Pentecost 16
Ordinary Time 23
    The Crux Of Being A Christian
    Luke 14:25-33

Proper 19   65
Pentecost 17
Ordinary Time 24
    God's Passionate Concern
    Luke 15:1-10

Proper 20   71
Pentecost 18
Ordinary Time 25
    Clever Christians
    Luke 16:1-13

Proper 21   79
Pentecost 19
Ordinary Time 26
    Keep Things Flowing
    Luke 16:19-31

Proper 22   85
Pentecost 20
Ordinary Time 27
    Nobody Owes You Anything
    Luke 17:5-10

Lectionary Preaching After Pentecost   91

Foreword

These talks come from the pen of the Reverend Richard W. Patt, pastor of a mission congregation in Tucson, Arizona.

I learned to know him as the pastor of a very large parish in the Midwest, and he took a call to be a pastor in a small congregation where he is able to do a lot of the things that he did not have time for in the past.

His talks have to do with little people with names like "Martha." Pastor Patt understands people like that. He is always doing, as Martha was. He received from the Lord a great story, as Martha did. It is Good News every step of the way. Reading these talks, like the one about the acceptance by Jesus of the invitation from Martha, people may say, "You mean He is *really coming*?"

As Pastor Patt puts it, the Good News is a real story about what really happened. The Son of God came, lived, died, and was raised from the dead by the glory of his Father. It is all for real. It is unquestionably true!

How great to have people telling that story these days! How great to believe it! How great to tell it again and again! How great to love as God loves! How great to be the light of the world! How great to be the salt of the earth bearing the Name of Jesus Christ!

How great to know Jesus Christ and the power of His resurrection! Pastor Patt digs into the Word of God, letting everybody know how great it is!

Oswald C.J. Hoffmann
Honorary Speaker
"The Lutheran Hour"

Preface

The theme of this book is taken from the title of the first sermon, "All Stirred Up." I hope that all of the sermons will "stir" the reader in at least two ways. I hope these sermons will stir you emotionally. That is, I hope that reading these sermons will frequently leave you slightly agitated in the sense that you feel shaken anew by some of the words and actions of Jesus. At times I hope these sermons will catapult you into having some creative mental arguments with me, or with the fascinating characters in these Gospel stories, not the least of which is Jesus himself. These sermons can only be considered productive when they cause you to reconsider the old truths in a new light. I hope these sermons make the familiar stories they are based on (mostly the parables of Jesus) pleasingly fresh in your mind and heart. I hope you will be so "stirred."

But I further hope that these sermons will stir you in another way. I would like them to leave you "all stirred up" about the gospel of Jesus Christ and about the enterprise of proclaiming it at this particular time. Many pastors will read this book. I hope their reading will bring them a new excitement and positive commitment about the gospel. I hope these sermons will increase their desire to preach the gospel!

Together with the pastors I hope all others who read these sermons will be stirred toward redoubling their efforts for the mission of the church as this century draws to an end. After 37 years of preaching, I thank God that I still remain stirred by it all myself!

I want to thank my secretary, Dorothy Pufahl, for her expertise in helping produce this manuscript.

Richard W. Patt
Tucson, Arizona
September 1, 1996

All Stirred Up

Proper 11 *Luke 10:38-42*
Pentecost 9
Ordinary Time 16

All stirred up — that's the way you sometimes feel. Agitated, nervous, worked up, wound up — for whatever reason. One feature in the story before us is that Jesus appeared to be responsible for bringing one of his dearest friends to such a point of agitation.

If you read the Bible carefully, you shouldn't be completely surprised about this. Jesus often left people stirred up. The religious leaders were frequently angered by his words and actions. His miracles left onlookers stirred to the point of awe and wonder. Some of his words left his own disciples nervous and on edge.

Jesus always had a *salutary* goal in stirring up people. His aims were never vicious. In their agitated state, Jesus wanted people to think more seriously about what he was saying or doing. He often wanted people to reorder their priorities. In the final analysis, his motives were *good*. After all he came to bring good news, a more abundant life, and a greater sense of personal serenity. Christ came not to destroy, but to save. Let's see how his noble purpose works out in your life and mine.

In a way, it's surprising that Saint Luke included this incident in his gospel at all. It doesn't serve to advance the greater drama of Luke's gospel story. At this time Jesus was on his way to

Jerusalem, where those climactic events that spelled his condemnation and crucifixion would soon unfold. Next to all of that, this visit with Mary and Martha appears incidental.

This is part of the story's charm. Here is Jesus, about to undergo as heavy a human agenda as one could imagine, stopping in for a visit with friends! Even when the major challenge of his ministry and life looms before him, Christ is found in the center of humble human activity. He is dropping in on friends. God's "got the whole world in his hands," as the old folk song puts it, yet God never loses interest in each one of us. God's willing to spend time with us. You and I are part of God's continuing concern.

Now I suspect, however, that it was Martha who initiated this encounter. The Bible writer leaves the fact open by saying "a woman named Martha received him into her house." No doubt the news traveled that Jesus was in the area. Martha enjoyed entertaining in her house, it seems. When the prospect of hosting the popular rabbi from Nazareth arose, we can imagine that she jumped at the chance. She was probably the proactive initiator of the invitation. To her initial delight, Jesus accepted.

At this point must we not say a word of commendation about what Martha did? She was a front porch person — willing to open her porch and her home for the sake of extending hospitality when it was needed. Jesus was on the road, and his agenda was consuming. Since he accepted the invitation, he must have felt a need for rest and restoration. Martha provided him that.

We live in an age when just about all human contact has to be scheduled. Why? Because more and more we force ourselves into situations where we are encapsuled and, therefore, unavailable. Our homes are electronically gated. In apartments and condominiums our entrances are unapproachable. Our air-controlled cars mean windows up; even our telephones are equipped with screening that implies, "You may call me if you want, but I'll have to get back to you." There are few front porches left. We allow limited access into most parts of our lives. Is it allowable to pop in on anyone any more? Hurray for Martha! She was accessible; she thereby provided for the Lord's human need.

Sad to say, her best intentions turned into a sour situation. It was not too long before she felt all stirred up. This blessed, felicitous woman had set out to do a noble deed. But soon the air was full of tension. How did all this develop?

It developed when the *task* involved in the venture overwhelmed her. Martha invited Jesus to stop by her home and he accepted. "He did? He accepted? You mean he is *really coming*?" It's like the little schoolboy who comes home from school on Monday afternoon, the day when Sunday leftovers usually are served for supper, and announces that he invited the school principal for supper, *and she's coming*! We all have the best of intentions in our moments of cordiality, but then it dawns on us that being cordial sometimes involves a little work and preparation. Maybe that's why the story in the Bible here doesn't refer to *Mary* and Martha's home. It simply says "her house," referring to Martha alone. She was well-known for supplying a delicious impromptu spread on the table. Everybody enjoyed going to "her house."

But that's what got her in trouble. Her heart led her head, and now she would have to do something about it. An awesome menial task stared her in the face. She had a table to spread. Company was coming, and she had invited them.

So this potentially beautiful occasion quickly grew ugly. While she was busy in the kitchen, Mary, her sister, chose to remain with Jesus in the living room, listening to his words of wisdom. Martha wanted everything in the kitchen to turn out just right. Sometimes striving for perfection spells pressure. The resulting tension can drive us to search for an explanation — even for blame. That's exactly what Martha did. She wondered whether her sister appreciated the tension she was under in the kitchen. In fact, she surmised, if her sister had the sense to come and help, most of the burden could be eased. Then, in her mind, Jesus also becomes part of the problem, as she bursts into the living room with her accusatory question, "Lord, do you not care that my sister has left me to serve alone?" Without waiting for an answer, she orders Jesus, "Tell her then to help me."

Martha and her reactions would make a good laboratory case for a beginner's course in psychology. This is a story about stress and its anatomy. We can dissect it. Stress is a neutral factor. It can lead us to heights of creativity, or it can drag us down to a point where we become an ugly, accusatory, blaming sort of person headed for defeat. Stress can lead us one way or another.

Sometimes we hear a woman say, "You know I *enjoy* having all the family over and cooking a big meal." Or we hear a young man say, "I enjoy my job; every day I walk into work, it's a challenge." What both of these persons are saying is something we rarely say outright, *that we actually welcome a degree of stress in our lives.* Right! Let's not make the six-letter word "stress" a four-letter word. Stress needn't be all negative. A lot of it can be positive, producing the good kind of adrenaline that opens the road to abundant creativity and achievement. And who doesn't enjoy achieving? For most of us it's a need we love to fulfill.

That's the way it could have been for Martha. But she forgot who it was she had invited! The honored guest was not some cold, egotistical citizen who needed to be impressed. This was *Jesus,* whose life's motto was known to everyone: "I have come, not to be served, but to serve." By this time Jesus had established a pattern in his ministry which let everyone know he was approachable. He liked nothing more than simply to sit down and share a good story. He was a people person who valued the delights of human interchange and genuine hospitality. In such a fertile context he knew that people could let their guards down, share their burdens, exchange their joys, announce their dreams, and be open to healing. If a little food and drink could be mixed in — fine. Spread the tablecloth. Martha forgot that Jesus was not a very demanding guest.

It's in this connection that Jesus makes his comment about Mary, the other sister. "Martha, Martha," he says, "you are anxious and troubled about many things; one thing is needful. Mary has chosen the good portion, which shall not be taken away from her" (vv. 41-42).

"One thing is needful." What is needful is that human beings regularly find themselves in a *productive* atmosphere that brings nurture and encouragement to their lives. We do not live "by bread alone." We live — and thrive and soar to the heights — when we come to greater insights and understanding about life and how to live it abundantly. Here was Jesus, the bread of life, present and available. Martha had her mind on other bread. "Martha was distracted," the story says, "with much serving" (v. 40).

So Martha missed out hearing the stimulating words that fell from the Master's lips. Did you ever wonder what Mary and Jesus were discussing in the living room? The story doesn't say exactly. Considering the context in which Jesus was traveling, making his way to Jerusalem and the Passover, he may have been giving Mary a preview of his coming struggle and passion. In that regard he may have been further interpreting these events for her — how the cross and his death were part of God's plan for the world's salvation, and how the Father in heaven would bring all of this to a salutary ending in the resurrection on the third day. What food, what bread — the Master himself giving a personal, unerring interpretation about all the ambiguous events that were about to happen! Who would have wanted to miss out on that?

Whenever we sit with the Lord, he brings us insight and understanding, not only about his own suffering and struggle, but about our own as well. When you and I feel nervous and agitated, worked up and wound up because of what's going on in our lives, we need an understanding partner with whom to sit down, so that we can sort things out, gain an understanding of our situation, and receive encouraging words from the person listening.

But it can be tough to come by such agreeable, healing situations for two reasons: first, the people we *could* sit down with are not always accessible, not available; or second, we are pressed and stressed to the point where we are consumed by our own activities, and therefore *we* are unavailable to sit down and put ourselves in an atmosphere of encouragement and healing. Martha had an accessible porch, and she even succeeded in getting the right guest into the living room, but then she herself insisted on being unavailable for the potential blessing that might have been hers.

By the way, don't you think Luke also included this incident in his gospel account because he found it irresistible — or perhaps more accurately — because he found a touch of *humor* in it? There *is* humor here, isn't there? We smile at the story because we see ourselves in it, or we detect someone we know who is similar to Martha. Sometimes our priorities, or frustrations, are so far off the beam that they are laughable. And along with this was Martha's own lack of humor, which might have finally saved her. "The Lord's coming to my house? You mean he *did* accept my reckless invitation?" Martha might have asked. "Well, then, he's going to have to settle for potluck!" Such an attitude *could* have made Martha a relaxed, delightful hostess.

A friend of mine likes to tell stories about how his teenage children would call him at home on the telephone on Friday nights after the high school basketball games. It was usually about 10 o'clock and they wanted to know whether they could bring a few friends over for a little get-together. When the parents asked how many friends were coming, they were usually told, "Oh, about seventeen." Instead of slamming down the phone, the guy said he always smiled at his wife, and the two of them hightailed it over to the supermarket to get enough supplies to feed and water down the two dozen teenagers who showed up. The slight ridiculousness of the situation and the parents' humorous response to it preserved a loving relationship between them and their children.

Finally, this story seems to suggest that Martha, at bottom line, was in a frazzle, because, after all, *the Lord Jesus Christ himself* was present in her living room. Despite all her mixed priorities, despite the way she fell victim to stress and its wiles, she probably never would have totally avoided the tenseness of the situation, for (think of it) none other than the Savior himself was a guest at her table!

There is an allowable kind of awe that any of us ought to feel in the Lord's presence. If such awe results in feeling overwhelmed and on edge, that is all right. After all, we are creatures, and God is creator. The Lord is holy and we are sinners. God is eternal, and we are dust. There are times when we ought to be "still and know that God is God."

In a worship service we can feel both. We can take off our shoes, for we stand on holy ground. And we can *kick* off our shoes and sit back, and we can revel in his healing presence. Christ has paid the price for our sins. He has died on the cross for us. He is the risen Savior of Easter who has won us a place in heaven. The work of salvation is finished. In Christ, God is now our friend. We can sit down with him, because he deigns to tarry with us. Welcome him into your home; welcome him into your heart. Do not miss the chance of dwelling in the Lord's healing presence!

It's Okay
To Stir Up God

Proper 12 *Luke 11:1-13*
Pentecost 10
Ordinary Time 17

Sometimes you and I have to stoke up enough nerve to ask someone for a favor. We find it tough to ask for something — for *anything*. I'm not thinking about asking someone for a large sum of money either. It can be as simple as asking for a ride when our own car is temporarily out of commission, or asking someone at a dinner table to pass us the potatoes. We are inclined to hesitate when it comes to asking favors of others, even small ones.

This is probably the case for at least two reasons. First, we tend to be fiercely independent. We want to do things on our own. In the second place, we fear that others might view us as being inadequate if we have to ask for something, even when the predicament is quite understandable. Along with these two reasons there is a general, vague feeling that we don't want to be a bother to someone else.

Sometimes prayer means asking for something. For that reason alone, people may hesitate to pray. When they consider that it is God they are addressing in their prayer, they may become doubly hesitant. In the gospel story before us, Jesus wants to assure us that we have permission to pray! More than that, he's telling us that it's okay to "bother" God, even stir up God, if need be, when we come to him in prayer.

Is there something in your heart you'd like to ask God about; something you'd like to ask him *for*? Jesus would say, "Go ahead; don't hesitate; don't be embarrassed. Take it to the Lord in prayer!" Let's listen as Jesus talks about all this. The outline to guide us is threefold: 1) the **promise** of prayer; 2) the **reality** of prayer; and 3) the **practice** of prayer.

The Promise Of Prayer

Despite the fact that you and I may hesitate about asking for *anything* — even in prayer — we ought to be encouraged about coming to God in prayer when we realize the **promise** of prayer. We do lots of things in life when a promise — and dare we say, sometimes a reward — is connected to them! Children are typically motivated about carrying out a request when some reward is promised. But we are all that way! With the right promise behind it, we will pursue even a disagreeable prospect.

The attractive promise that Jesus announces here is that as we pray we ought to take into consideration that God is on our side. That's an encouraging truth, isn't it? God is on our side! Let's look at the concluding verses of this text first. Notice the imagery Jesus uses to bring us this good news. In verses 11-13 Jesus appeals to our reasoning power when he asks, "What father among you, if his son asks for a fish, will instead of a fish give him a serpent; or if he asks for an egg, will give him a scorpion? If you then, who are evil, know how to give good gifts to your children, how much more will the heavenly Father give the Holy Spirit to those who ask him!"

Yes, even a human father doesn't usually treat his children cruelly. If that's true, think of how much more the heavenly Father desires to bless us all. In other words, Jesus wants us to be convinced that God is unquestionably on our side. From the beginning of our prayer, God is ready to listen for the sake of bringing us the best possible blessing. What a promise!

Even before we get set to pray, haven't you and I previously experienced God's good intentions toward us? Look at the marvelous world God has given us by God's creative power. God didn't give us a stripped-down, boring universe. On the contrary, our world of landscapes and the universe of planets and stars constantly invigorate us with their beauty and agreeable surprises. God could have had us live minimally; instead we are constantly surrounded by a variety that brings spice to life. God gives us extras; God is on our side!

The First Article of the Creed tells us as much. But it is in the Second Article, where we confess Jesus Christ as Savior, that we come to realize in the most profound way that God is on our side. The Second Article leads us into the uttermost region of God's heart. There we find a heart ready and willing to forgive us. So much is God on our side that even when we deserve being rejected by God and condemned, God takes a path that forgives and restores us.

All of this God does because of Jesus Christ. His suffering for our sins, his death for our guilt, and his resurrection on Easter Day are positive signs of God's commitment to you and me. We have a Father who will not let us go! He will not let us down! In the eighth chapter of the book of Romans, Saint Paul verbalizes this wonder: "There is therefore now no condemnation for those who are in Christ Jesus." Paul crowns this thought later in the chapter in the triumphant question: "If God is *for us*, who is against us?" The promise of prayer is that you *can* pray, you are *invited* to pray, you are *encouraged*, if need be, to storm the gates of heaven with your prayers. After all, God is on your side.

I believe that, as human beings, this is just the truth we are waiting to hear. A few years ago on television, a public speaker was giving a talk about the three deepest needs we have as persons. What would you imagine those to be? The first need we have, the speaker said, is to know someone who will listen to us. We all have a story to tell, a need to verbalize our feelings. We want someone who will *listen* to that. Secondly, he claimed, we want the person listening to *believe* what we are saying. We want someone who will trust our story. Finally, the television speaker said that when we have found such a person who listens to us and trusts us, we want to be assured that such a person *is on our side*. We don't want to be involved with someone who will misuse or abuse our story (through gossip, for instance), but who will remain on our side, perhaps despite our story.

From personal experience I'd say the speaker touched on an important aspect of our deepest need as people. The promise of prayer — of Christian prayer — is that for the sake of Jesus Christ our Savior, a loving Father is ready to listen to you and me; as God listens, we may be assured that God is on our side all the way. This is the promise of prayer.

The Reality Of Prayer

So now that we realize the promise of prayer, it is time to move on to the **reality** of prayer. It's easy for most of us to have someone encourage us about praying. But then we ask, "What do I do now? How do I go about praying?" The disciples in this story must have felt similarly lacking. In the opening verse here it says that one of them came to Jesus, who had just finished praying, and asked him, "Lord, teach us to pray...." Like us, they too wanted to know about the reality of prayer.

When Jesus responded by giving them the words we now know as the Lord's Prayer, I believe his goal was more general than specific. Though the words have turned out to be *the* classic prayer of Christendom, I believe that Jesus initially intended them to portray the *spirit* of our prayers instead of specified words. Look closely at the Lord's Prayer sometime. What it expresses is an attitude about how we're going to think of God and how we're going to live our lives. Jesus is making it clear here that prayer is *a way of living* more than it is a daily ritual of words. The apostle Paul affirmed such an approach when he wrote the famous brief sentence, "Pray without ceasing." Part of what he meant by that involves the thought that all of our lives ought to be a prayer to God. The sense of living in God's presence should be an ongoing reality in our lives.

Most of us have heard something about learning how to pray when one finds oneself in a foxhole. The expression arose out of the Second World War, when many a soldier had to take refuge from bombs and bullets by lying in trenches called foxholes. With explosions taking place all around, a soldier, it was surmised, learned quickly how to pray, how to plead for safety and God's care while enemy fire was blazing overhead.

Who wouldn't pray when the troubles and disasters of life are inundating us? But far better it is to be living in a spirit of prayer at *every* time of life. That's what Jesus is trying to teach the disciples here when he gives them the treasured words of the Lord's Prayer: live every moment knowing that a loving heavenly Father is on your side. Hallow God's name by realizing that all of life is hallowed and sacred. God's kingdom is always among us, and every time is the right time to live according to God's will. Realize further that God will always supply the daily bread you need. Live in forgiveness and peace with all others, because in the cross of Christ God has forgiven you, too. Don't put yourself in situations where you could be tempted to sin. Don't make it unduly difficult for God to deliver you from evil. Acknowledge God's sovereignty and stand in awe of God's kingdom, power, and glory. Live all of your life as a prayer to the Lord. Then you will be praying the Lord's Prayer, even though you are not mouthing the words. The reality of prayer is that praying is a way of life more than it is a daily ritual of words.

The Practice Of Prayer

Nevertheless, prayer is often a ritual of words. It is a ceremonial practice of the people of God. It is a daily act that is worthwhile. What does Jesus teach us then, finally, about the *practice* of prayer?

First of all, Jesus allows for the fact that prayer might become a habit. Consider this: when Jesus first gave these disciples the Lord's Prayer, do you think he realized what a habit those words would become? The Lord's Prayer is now the universal prayer of the Church. It is part of our historic liturgies and forms a climactic element in the consecration of the Holy Communion. We say the prayer at baptisms and make it a part of most public church services. Our children learn these words at an early age. Most Christians I know say the prayer at least once a day. The Lord's Prayer is part and parcel of Christian piety. In other words, among people of the Church, the Lord's Prayer has become a habit.

But what a good habit it is! Could our children learn any better words than these as they pray? When you and I become speechless in our prayers, unable to verbalize what is on our minds, this supreme prayer says it all for us. I brush my teeth and eat some food every day, even as I engage in dozens of other good habits every day. Maybe our Lord surmised that we needed one prayer that would overtake our hearts and minds and be so treasured among us that it would become second nature to us. Personally, I thank God for the good habit of knowing and saying the Lord's Prayer every day. Pastors who visit patients with Alzheimer's disease frequently report that when such patients seem to exhibit no awareness or understanding of what is going on at the moment, they *do* immediately join in and pray aloud with the minister as those familiar words are intoned, "Our Father, who art in heaven...." Prayer itself, and the Lord's Prayer, can be a sustaining habit.

Along with this thought, is it not true that most of us require some kind of structure in the practice of prayer? The prayers that others have prayed can give structure and content to our own prayers. Go ahead and pray the Lord's Prayer. Its author is the most exquisite teacher the Church has ever had! And how about the treasure of the psalms? These 150 songs of faith contain something for everyone. If you don't know exactly what to pray or how to say it, one of the psalms will give you the words and thoughts for which you are searching. Published prayers in countless books and collections have voiced the petitions of God's people down through the ages. Prayer books will not assure you of taking time to pray, but they will give you something worthwhile to say when you take time to pray. With the Bible and various prayer books at hand, you will probably be more apt to take them in hand and use them! Commit yourself to a time or to several times a day when you will pray.

But the feature about prayer that Jesus wishes to impress us about above all can be stated succinctly: *pray with persistence.* Never give up asking God for his blessings. Never give up coming to God in faith and trust. Never give up asking.

Jesus tells a charming parable to make this point. A man receives a surprise visitor at midnight. The person needs a place to lodge overnight. In the times when this story was told, the average citizen viewed his duty in such a situation as being fairly compelling. People avoided traveling in the heat of the day; sometimes they wouldn't reach a feasible place to stop until late in the evening. Only the most hardened soul would have the heart to turn down a friend under such circumstances. So the friend is invited in, but the host has no food to offer. So the host knocks on the door of his neighbor/friend, asking for some bread. The neighbor/friend turns down the request of providing bread at this hour. Again, we have to appreciate a practice of the times. Both were probably modest homes. These homes usually had only one large room, multipurpose in use. When the daytime activities of the family were concluded, the living area was recycled into a sleeping area for everyone. During the daytime the single door into the home stood open, signaling to visitors that they were welcome, for the room had not yet been rearranged for sleeping. But once the room was prepared for bedtime, the door was shut, meaning that everyone in the house was now settled for the night in tight quarters. To fumble about and prepare three loaves of bread in such limited space would probably mean waking up the whole brood of children, thus upsetting the household for the rest of the night.

So it is that the neighbor answers the embarrassed host, "Do not bother me; the door is now shut, and my children are with me in bed; I cannot get up and give you anything" (v. 7). But here we have a host who is so desperate that the commonly accepted closed door signal means nothing to him. He knocks and knocks, again and again. Then Jesus comments about how this petitioner's persistence will eventually press the neighbor until he gives in and shells out the bread. Jesus further comments that the same kind of persistence in prayer is admirable.

Now we have come full circle in our consideration of this text. Why should we dare to be so persistent in our prayers? Why should we even go to the lengths of "stirring up" God, as this man in the story stirred up his neighbor/friend at midnight? Because God is on our side; God has our needs at heart. God understands the predicaments of life. He is probably even impressed when our prayers are not for our own sake but for someone else whose needs we have adopted as our own. We should be persistent because when we have banked on God and God's goodness all along in our lives, there is no reason to stop trusting God and believing in God when we are in a jam. In fact, especially then God will be the good Father who knows what gift will be best for us.

We live in a time when people seem to have given up such hope and trust. Little in life seems worthwhile; much of life doesn't seem worth the effort. Some are not only resigned *to* the future, but they have also resigned *from* the future. Their forward thrust is gone. Faith has petered out. Prayer appears to be an anachronism. But this parable encourages us to keep stirring up God until he gives us an ear.

Bil Keane, who draws the popular *Family Circus* cartoons, portrays a father who is fast asleep on the living room couch, his back facing outward and his face buried in the pillows. Anticipating being bothered by his little boy about who-knows-what, this father has cleverly pinned a paper sign across his back that reads, "Go ask Mommy." The little tyke, unable to read, does just what his dad hopes he won't do: he tugs and tugs at his dad's shirt, asking the question, "What does that sign say, Daddy? Daddy?"

Two points for us: number one, hurray for the little guy, who feels it proper to come and approach his father under any circumstance. Number two, God, thanks be, doesn't need the sleep the father seemed to need. We are not a bother to God — ever! We never come to God alone as God's child. We come with Christ, and in the name of Christ, and that makes all the difference in the world.

Rich In God's Sight

Proper 13 *Luke 12:13-21*
Pentecost 11
Ordinary Time 18

The key verse of the parable Jesus tells here has a way of sending a chill down the spine. In that verse God exclaims, "Fool! This night your soul is required of you ..." (v. 20). Hearing that dramatic warning, maybe you have surmised, "Will I ever get caught in a situation where those stern words are addressed to *me*?"

Generally we tend to feel we have our lives on the right track. We try to keep a pleasing balance between material things and the things of the spirit. But when we look objectively, we *are* concerned about our own security — both for the present and the future. Frankly, we have money on our minds more than we'd like to admit. Often these material concerns are so pervasive that in honesty we would have to agree that God might be justified in surprising us with the indictment here: "Fool! This night your soul is required of you!"

The plain fact is that a lot of the time our soul's concern is not about being rich in God's sight, but about being rich, period — or at least financially secure. Jesus pulls no punches here when he points out that all of us at our demise will end up empty-handed anyway, and that at bottom line the only wealth that will count is whether we are "rich toward God," as he puts it.

Jesus drives home his point by telling a story we know as "The Parable of the Rich Fool." In the story Jesus tells about a wealthy man, which in his day would probably mean a successful farmer. Crops, barns; more crops, more barns. In our day Jesus might have used characters like folks who are consumed in the stock market or other investments; or those addicted to gambling, or even a young married couple who will do almost anything (like neglecting one another or their children) in order to ascend to the next rung on the ladder of monetary success.

At any rate, the hour for calling the question draws closer and closer for every human being. Finally, BAM! The symbolic barns we have been building are toppled. Time runs out, and we hear the voice say, "Fool! This night your soul is required of you." The question being called, of course, is this: Rich? or rich *in God's sight*?

You and I do not have to have Jesus draw us a picture (as he did in this parable) in order to realize the folly of thinking that life is only a matter of money, or of the security such funds provide. We are the people of God; we know the supreme blessings involved in being "rich in God's sight." So that is what we want to consider in a positive way: being rich — being rich in God's sight.

As we consider the parable, the first point that impresses us is the story's sense of urgency. Time marches on. The days and years tick away. There are certain things that ought to be done before time runs out.

Being rich in God's sight means first of all our realization that there is a spiritual urgency about life. That urgency primarily involves our own eternal salvation. In the Gospels Jesus' initial message was the same as John's clarion call: "Repent, for the kingdom of God is *near!*" Though Jesus dealt with people in a patient manner, one can sense an urgency about everything he said and did. There is an opportune time. There is a day of salvation.

Many of the hymns of Christianity stir us in regard to the urgency of our eternal salvation. "Delay not, delay not, O sinner draw near ... delay not, delay not, the hour is at hand." The Advent hymns breathe the urgency too: "Prepare the royal highway; the King of kings is near! Let every hill and valley a level road appear!" Or how about the old Gospel hymn:

> *Softly and tenderly Jesus is calling,*
> *calling for you and for me;*
> *Time is now fleeting, the moments are passing,*
> *passing for you and for me.*

There are spiritual urgencies concerning our salvation that we need to tend to!

Does not this urgency also have to do with the Christian enterprise — the Christian mission? The very word "mission" has a ring of urgency about it. We are "rich in God's sight" when we are fairly consumed by this mission. We are rich when we are proclaiming the riches of God's love in Christ to others. Again the hymn writers inspire us toward the call: "Stand up, stand up for Jesus, as soldiers of the cross, lift high the royal banner, it must not suffer loss." Harry Emerson Fosdick stated the urgency long ago in a verse of his hymn, "God Of Grace And God Of Glory." He writes:

> *Rich in things and poor in soul: Grant us wisdom, grant us courage lest we miss your kingdom's goal; lest we miss your kingdom's goal.*

Or how about the urgency of striving toward Christian values? In our time there is a lot of talk about the loss of human values, moral values, as they touch upon the home, marriage, and sexuality. Have we no more Christian values?

Of course we do! Most people I know of — and not especially those in the church, but including them, of course — have moral values that reflect the standards of the Ten Commandments. Our problem is not that we have lost our values, or that as Christians we have lost our sense of Christian missions. What we have lost is an *urgency* about these things. That is the heart of the story Jesus tells here, isn't it? The farmer lacked a sense of urgency. He didn't realize that time flies — and finally runs out. This farmer was no vicious unbeliever; few of us are. He was a *confused* farmer — confused about crops and barns and investments and security, and about what place such things should hold in his life.

A lot of destructive things happen today in our society because evil people are active in doing evil things. But equally true, a lot of evil is happening because many good people are doing nothing. A sense of urgency — of proactive goodness, if you will — escapes them. In theology it is called "sins of omission." In the liturgy we confess such sins of omission when we say, "We have sinned against you ... by what we have done *and by what we have left undone.*"

Whenever Christians say the Apostles' Creed they not only enunciate their Christian faith; they also proclaim their Christian values. For instance, when we say we believe in God the Father almighty, creator of heaven and earth, we affirm a gracious and loving God as the giver of the earth to us all. But we are also saying that we *value* the gift of the earth; we will care for it and be good stewards of it.

These Christian values not only need to be affirmed; they need to be put into practice. In fact in our day there is an urgency about the need to care for the earth. Yes, it is the environmental concern, and it is front burner stuff. We have gotten rich off the earth but have not been "rich toward God," as Jesus says, in treasuring the earth by avoiding its misuse and abuse.

Our sense of urgency in this regard needs to push us toward intentional action. For example, people who highly value God's creation will quietly go about the proper recycling of their paper and plastic discards, their used motor oil and anything else that has a potential for harming the environment. Such concerned people will increasingly become sensitive consumers, carefully weighing what to buy or whether they need to buy certain products at all. Lovers of God's creation will teach their children and grandchildren at an early age about the sacredness of the land. They will implement their sense of values about the creation by sometimes casting their vote with those political candidates who share similar values. They will, in short, not allow lesser souls to continue painting the world into a corner until its fatal condition becomes irreversible. Yes, to be "rich toward God" means ultimately standing as sentinels over the riches of the earth God made. May the day never come when God will be forced to stand over the planet and lament toward its inhabitants, "Fool! This night your soul is required of you!"

Speaking of souls, what about the souls of our children, our youth? As we express our Christian values in the creed, we need to communicate these values to our children and youth, as another sign that we are rich in God's sight. The souls of young people are precious, partly because they contain such fertile ground, soil filled with the potential of becoming rich toward God. What productive souls await God and the church in our own children! They stand there, just waiting to have their values formed.

How much more could a Christian be considered "rich in God's sight" than to be able to say, "I helped a young person come to know Christ; I did what I could to bring Christian values to the young people of my church." Children will generally follow effective leaders. They will listen to those who take time to listen to them. They stand on tiptoe in their desire to make meaningful commitments. Young people are ready; they are always standing near the edge of responding. They are eager souls.

But at this point a lot of adult persons would claim that they *have* a heart for children, their own and youth generally. Concerned adult Christians would further point out that they *do* feel an urgency about the whole matter. Indifference is not their problem. But a problem does plague them: they feel *inadequate* about communicating with youth; they don't know how to bring Christian values to children — even to their own.

Two points in response are these. Number one, when you don't know how to do a job, you seek training. Bringing our children to faith is a job, and it is our job. In fact, it is one of the features of the vocation of Christian parenthood. Christian parents need to seek training in caring for the souls of their children, and the church needs to provide the training. Number two, there are plenty of gifted young adults and adults who are expert in sharing the faith with children. Christians who see the urgency will provide for such expert leadership in their church congregations. They will get outside help.

All such things, of course, involve time and money. To be "rich in God's sight" means that Christians will literally pay the cost involved in the urgent mission of bringing faith and Christian values to their children and to all children and youth of the church, and, pray God, to many outside the church. Pastors these days hear the frequent observation voiced that their congregations are increasingly made up of gray heads. The unspoken projection assumed in such an observation is that someday there may be nothing but gray heads worshiping in the churches. Perhaps it could come to that. At that point, one can again imagine the divine exclamation that would send a shiver down the spine. "Fool! This night your soul is required of you!"

Urgency! That's the theme of the parable here. And the flip side of it all — the side that brings us an encouraging and enabling word — involves the grateful realization that God once regarded *our* salvation and rescue as being urgent. God was not indifferent to the plight of God's children. God realized how close to the edge our sins had gotten us; how, indeed, we had become lost sheep, shepherdless and alone. With urgency, "while we were yet sinners," God dispatched a good shepherd among us. The shepherd went forth uncomplaining, leaving the ninety and nine, to find the one lost soul so far from the green pastures. Yes, this divine shepherd — wonder of all wonders — became a weak, powerless Lamb of God, and went to the plank and was crucified for us all. There is a divine urgency in God's love. Our Lord Jesus Christ did not delay in bringing us this kingdom of love. We are saved! We are rescued! We are now rich in God, with all the wealth of eternal life waiting for us. Now it is time to become rich *toward* God, rich in God's sight, as we position ourselves to extend God's riches to a waiting world.

The Fear
Of Taking The Plunge

Proper 14 *Luke 12:32-40*
Pentecost 12
Ordinary Time 19

In a lengthy paragraph just before this text Jesus told the disciples to relax and enjoy life as it comes to them. Many of the phrases in that speech have become legendary: "... do not be anxious about your life ... which of you by being anxious can add a cubit to his span of life? ... Consider the lilies, how they grow; they neither toil nor spin...." In short Jesus was coaxing the disciples with the appeal, "Let go, and let God."

But after saying all that, Jesus realized that such appeals scare most of us half to death. So he adds those comforting words: "Fear not, little flock, for it is your Father's good pleasure to give you the kingdom." Jesus enjoins the disciples not to get hung up on fear as he issues yet another drastic appeal: "Sell your possessions, and give alms...."

What were the disciples afraid of? They were afraid of the same thing you and I are — of taking the plunge. They were scared to death, and so are we, when asked to neutralize their lives to the point that they are depending on God as much as they were on their assets. In fact, Jesus suggested that they reconfigure their lives to the extent that they were totally depending on God and his goodness. Such a prospect frightened them to no end. So, first of all, Jesus encouraged them here, "Fear not, little flock."

Jesus tried to bring some rationale to his appeal by reminding the disciples that by taking such a plunge they will then be basing their future welfare on "a treasure in the heavens *that does not fail,* where no thief approaches and no moth destroys." Jesus was suggesting that, unlike banking on their own possessions (which are unpredictable), they can have a totally predictable future by relying on God's never-failing fatherly care.

The Scandinavian philosopher of the last century, Soren Kierkegaard, called it "the leap of faith." Today let's just call it "taking the plunge," and then ask the question: "Why is there so much fear about that?"

The obvious reason for our fear of taking the plunge is that we trust in our own assets more than we do in God's promises. Note the word "promise." Frankly most of us have difficulty believing anything could be much more promising than the status quo. We surmise: If something isn't broken, why fix it? But the fact is that in many respects people today do regard their current lot as being precisely that: fragmented, broken, disgustingly status quo and going nowhere. Longing to walk in the sweet-smelling lilies of the field, they continue groveling in the paralyzing pollution of their own anxiety: *They are afraid to move.*

That last statement can be taken quite literally. I once was in a conversation where one person in the group announced that he and his wife were moving to a more remote area of the state. Immediately others in the group objected, sounding as though they feared for the couple's well-being. These were the questions they asked: How can you give up the familiarity of this town? How do you know you'll ever feel at home in the new place? Can you stand to be away from your friends? Will you find a house there as nice as the one you live in now? Will you adjust to new doctors and dentists and will such people even be accessible to you in that remote area? As one listening to all of this, it dawned on me that many of the people asking such questions were exhibiting a fear about routine change that bordered on paranoia. Frankly they appeared scared to death for this man and his wife.

In her book called *Dakota*, Kathleen Norris, a best-selling writer and poet, tells how she and her husband, also a writer, moved away from the heady literary atmosphere and advantages of New York City to one of the most remote towns in America, Lemmon, South Dakota. She relates how most of her friends were shocked by their contemplated move. The prospects for even reasonable survival as thinking persons seemed as remote as the little town they chose to live in. But Kathleen Norris subtitled her book "A Spiritual Geography," because it was in that sparse geography that she found her own spirit more than ever. In Lemmon, South Dakota, she blossomed as the person and writer she suspected she could be. Most of her self-discovery was pleasing *and would have been impossible* had she insisted on remaining in the "safe" literary environment of New York. Jesus says, "Fear not, little flock, for it is your Father's good pleasure to give you the kingdom," and we might add, "kingdoms you never dreamed possible." People find this out when they take the plunge. What are we afraid of?

So hear this word again! "Fear not, little flock, for it is your Father's good pleasure to give you the kingdom." What is this *kingdom*? Jesus never crisply defines it for us anywhere in the Gospels. Nor does he here. But he always promises that the kingdom is a domain where God's grace and abundance can be experienced. Part of our typical limited view as human beings produces in us the conviction that the best of life is probably happening right now where *we* are, in *"our* little part of the kingdom," as we put it. We often bar ourselves from experiencing the exhilaration and challenge of a new kingdom by determining not to budge from the nice little setup we have concocted for ourselves. As a result, we fly low when we could be soaring. We hedge about believing that God "will bear us up on eagle's wings" when we take the plunge.

But Jesus adds another dimension to all of this when he introduces the idea about "being ready." He says, "Let your loins be girded and your lamps burning, and be like men who are waiting for their master to come home ..." (vv. 35-36). Then he adds, "You also must be ready" (v. 40). Ready for what? Ready to *move* somewhere? Perhaps. As we've said, it might not be a bad idea to be open to entertaining such a prospect as one option. Ready for the end? Yes, Jesus does seem to indicate something like that when he concludes this text with the words, "... the Son of Man is coming at an unexpected hour" (v. 40). Does not Jesus mean here that we should be prepared for *any and all* of the surprising opportunities of life — for those unplanned times when positive challenges and alternatives of life are thrust upon us?

Let us examine this thought in connection with one of the big negatives of life — the reality and presence of physical illness. Nobody welcomes physical illness; there is usually a jolting feeling connected with finding out we're ill. But I have come to discover that the person who has a regular pattern of daily commending life and limb to the Lord and his keeping is correspondingly able to handle illness well. In fact part of *getting* well is *handling* our illnesses well — handling all of life well, really, by allowing God to handle it: letting go and letting God.

Of course, I'm not saying here that faith overcomes all illness, but faith does carry us through our illnesses and any other challenge of life. In this connection, Jesus often introduced the imagery of storehouses into his conversations. He mentions such "storehousing" in the paragraph immediately before this text and in a parable earlier in the same chapter. Admittedly, when he was talking in those instances about putting things away for the future — storehousing — he was viewing the practice in a slightly negative way. But along with the idea of total faith in God, are there not *positive* kinds of storehousing you and I could be doing, so that we are *prepared* to meet some of the future occasions of life?

How about this matter of growing old, for instance? We could better meet the challenges of an aging body by being careful not to abuse the body in younger years. The same goes for the mind. The healthier and happier relationships are in younger years, the more joyous will be memories of them as we grow older. We will then have few regrets and will rest in the satisfaction that earlier days were filled with achievement and pleasure. We will grow older with a sense of fulfillment, not frustration. This positive kind of storehousing in earlier years will serve us well in later years.

Whether we realize it or not, our minds are automatic storehouses, not unlike any computer with the capacity for memory storing. For instance, things we literally memorize now can serve us well when life sends us a challenge. Dr. Walter W. Stuenkel, the retired president of Concordia University in Wisconsin, was well-known in the Milwaukee area for a particularly powerful element in his preaching. He had at his command literally thousands of Bible passages and traditional hymn verses — any of which he was able to bring to the surface at will, because he knew them all from memory! It aided his ability as a speaker immensely. But now, over 85 years old, living in retirement in Arizona, these thousands of literary treasures continue to be a blessing in his life as he devotionally recalls any and all of them for the sake of his own personal spiritual welfare and encouragement. Nothing can destroy and no moth can eat through his trusted storehouse! In a similar vein, I am acquainted with a host of elderly people whose poor eyesight makes it almost impossible for them to read Scripture or a hymnal anymore. But they too have a treasure of memorized Bible verses and hymns that they have known since childhood. They have instant recall of a valuable storehouse that brings comfort to their souls.

Elderly people also face the challenge of filling up the time at their disposal. But some of them have no trouble with that at all, because in earlier years they developed interest and expertise in a variety of cultural and mental activities that have now become a valuable storehouse upon which they draw. Music, literature, hobbies and arts fill their hours as they maintain a fascination with life and its rich spectrum of offerings. For them the plunge into retirement has not been half bad.

Not the least of the things that can prepare us to meet life's challenges is developing a rich cadre of friends. The old saying goes, "I get by with a little help from my friends." Sometimes that is all you need when the road gets bumpy — a few friends who will support and affirm you. Those who are wise have previously taken time to nurture and maintain friendships — that rich storehouse of other human beings with whom we can share the burdens that weigh us down (and, conversely, through whom we can sometimes get the attention off of ourselves by listening to *their* burdens and dreams). Conquering the frontier of aging becomes easier when we prepare for the plunge.

When you read through the Gospels carefully, you will note that Jesus was constantly forging new frontiers. He was not fearful about plunging into new territory. For him, as an example, illness was not something to which we always have to resign ourselves; we can challenge our sicknesses when we are open to God's healing power. The Gospel writers frequently point out that certain people with whom Jesus dealt were blind from birth or were physically disabled for decades, or they had a dreaded disease that was hopelessly incurable, like leprosy. Jesus took the leap of faith — or rather brought others to the point of taking a leap of faith — so that wholeness of life and limb nevertheless became a possibility.

Jesus also plunged into new territory by challenging some of the exclusivity of his native culture. He dared to believe that *all* people are children of the heavenly Father — even those in Samaria, even women, even Gentiles, even publicans and other sinners. While others stood in fear of acknowledging anyone outside the house of Israel, Jesus forthrightly embraced all persons as being in the fold of God's love. He could have been afraid; he should have been afraid, because by exhibiting such an open attitude he might end up being crucified some day. But Jesus did what he did because he had a vision of the kingdom; he knew it was his Father's good pleasure to give him a kingdom yet unknown: to bestow on all the world a future fellowship that was more grace-filled, more loving, more beautifully integrated and catholic than anyone had previously imagined or experienced. Yes, before its time Jesus had the vision of "one, holy, catholic church, the *communion* of saints."

All of this suggests that the church too could probably use a good dose of such pioneering spirit. The organization of the Church needs to take a leap of faith — perhaps a giant leap — in order to recapture the vision of one Church under the benevolent lordship of Jesus Christ. Much of the machinery of the Church today seems to be just that — machinery: toiling and spinning, anxious over maneuvering its own life and future. The Church needs to let go and let God!

All of this finally comes down to the stirring verse 34, where Jesus says in summary, "For where your treasure is, there will your heart be also." We know what our treasure is in the church. We place it at the center of our altars and at the top of our steeples everywhere. The *cross* is our jewel and the substance of everything for which we stand. It is "a treasure in the heavens that does not fail, where no thief approaches and no moth destroys." In the cross our salvation is signed, sealed, and delivered. Now it is our turn to take up the cross and follow him — even when it means taking the plunge.

Peace And
The Peacemakers

Proper 15　　　　　　　　　　　　　　　　　*Luke 12:49-56*
Pentecost 13
Ordinary Time 20

There are few other speeches of Jesus in the New Testament that catch us more off-guard than this one. Nobody would deny that these are some of the most intense words of Jesus that we find in the Bible. It would follow that any reader of these words, including those who believe in Jesus, would probably want some kind of explanation. Frankly, the Lord seems to be shouting at the top of his voice here. A little later we will talk about the deeper meaning behind the words that capture our ears here, phrases like, "I came to cast fire upon the earth," and "Do you think that I have come to give peace on earth? No, I tell you, but rather division...." Coming from Jesus, these words demand explanation, because we would expect Jesus to say the opposite of what we hear him saying here.

But for now let us try to understand these words in light of what was going on in Jesus' life at the time. That is true of all of us, isn't it? When something significant is going on in our lives, our demeanor and speech may reflect that. Our words, usually spoken calmly, may develop an unpleasing bite that betrays the fact that we're on edge. We understand that and allow for it in one another.

So we discover that the words of Jesus have a bite to them. He appears to be on edge. What's up? Jesus is worked up, that's what. His mind seems focused on the consuming event to come: his own crucifixion. Jesus often thought and spoke about that "hour." He knew that his mission on earth involved the cross. He would suffer and die for the sins of the world. That was his mission, and he knew the time was coming.

So, Jesus often had the cross in the back of his mind when he was speaking publicly or with his disciples. That seems to be the case here. He is talking with his disciples about living their lives in total commitment to God. The longer he talks about it, the more the subject excites him. All of a sudden he seems to shift the focus to himself, having reminded himself in his own conversation of the total commitment that was soon to be demanded of *him*! He realizes that his own nonviolent efforts to announce and proclaim the kingdom of God will soon result in violence that others will inflict upon him at the cross. These realities stir him deeply within. The disciples do not see all of this. They *couldn't* see it, and Jesus doesn't blame them for that. But the emotion of it sweeps over him and he spills forth:

> *I came to cast fire upon the earth; and would that it were already kindled! I have a baptism to be baptized with; and how I am constrained until it is accomplished! Do you think that I have come to give peace on earth? No, I tell you, but rather division."*   — Luke 12:49-51

Then he goes on to detail how houses will be divided and relatives set against one another. Strong words, dramatic images. Now we can understand a little why Jesus was stirred to this high pitch. The approaching hour of the cross was something Jesus had to live with from early on.

The second reason why Jesus was all worked up here is the fact that the "hour of the cross" was quickly approaching. Geographically speaking, at this juncture Jesus was making his final swing through territory that would land him in Jerusalem for his ultimate confrontation with his enemies, a confrontation that would directly lead to his crucifixion. In verses 54-56 Jesus (perhaps unduly) excoriates the multitude for not realizing that all of this was about to happen.

So this is a background that we need to appreciate as we hear these startling words from Jesus. When we look more closely there is a deeper meaning to these words, a meaning we urgently need to appreciate as people involved (as Jesus was) in proclaiming the Kingdom of God. We can get at this meaning by recalling that most of us would probably have expected Jesus to say exactly the opposite of what in fact he does say here. When Jesus says, "I came to cast fire upon the earth ..." wouldn't we have expected Jesus actually to have said, "I came to *put out* fire upon the earth"? Or when Jesus asks, "Do you think that I have come to give peace on earth?" most of us would have been inclined to answer, "Yes! Yes, peace instead of division, disunity, and a sword. Yes, *peace*, O Prince of Peace, and goodwill among people everywhere!"

So what is the meaning of all this, when in fact we hear Jesus announce that he came to bring fire upon the earth and division instead of peace? He meant to tell us that our mission of peacemaking will always bring the sword slingers out of the closet. He meant to tell us that those who work for unity will in the process have to go through conflicts that result in divisions and brokenness before the oneness emerges. Or as Jesus might put it, "I have come as the Savior of the world, but in the process of bringing salvation, 'I have a baptism to be baptized with; and how I am constrained until it is accomplished!' "

Unfortunately, history is filled with paradigms of this truth. Dr. Martin Luther King, Jr., attempted to bring unity to the *United States* of America, and he sought to do it through nonviolent means. We call this social oneness "integration." Yes, he sought to make America a nation of *integrity*. But the process of fulfilling his dream, as we well know, involved division, the sword, and his own assassination. Before him and after him came two other assassinations. John F. Kennedy and Robert F. Kennedy both died for the vision of seeing America rise above its divisions and become *one* nation under God.

In the Church's own history there have always been those heroes of faith who have suffered martyrdom in the cause of bringing the peace of the Gospel in a hostile world. Back in the year 1170 Thomas Becket was literally murdered in a cathedral at the hands of King Henry II in England because he refused to tolerate Henry's cry of "peace, peace," where there was no peace. Most of the apostles of Jesus himself were martyred at the hands of those who became unnerved by these messengers of peace. Those whose mission was to bring the peace of God often brought the sword upon themselves through no fault of their own; they brought a fire upon the earth that frequently consumed their own lives.

We know the reason for these disastrous responses to the proclamation of the Gospel. The reason is that a division of sorts boils within the heart of every human being. We are people filled with pride and self-serving. We become easily stuck on ourselves — stuck on the way *we* look, the way *we* do things, the culture and practices of life that *we* have developed and have come to hold so dear, the foods *we* eat and the neighborhoods *we* live in, *and* the protective economic network we have devised for ourselves and for those who are like us and who go along with our ways. People have a way of becoming so stuck on themselves that they will fight for their prejudices at the expense of civil rights; they will endure fire and the sword to insulate themselves against those they consider invaders of their turf. Stuck on themselves, it is difficult, if not impossible, for them to honor anyone else.

You know how Jesus had to deal with that in his day. We have to deal with it in our day as well. And the Church of Jesus Christ ought to deal with it, for only the Church possesses a power that can break down such walls between people. What we treasure in Word and Sacrament is nothing less than God's transforming power that finally gets the focus off ourselves and gives us the grace to be sensitive toward those who are different from us in any way. What only the Church possesses is the message of the cross, and the cross is the power of God unto salvation to everyone who believes. In the cross, we are saved *from* ourselves, first of all. We are no longer stuck on our selfish viewpoints. The cross burns that all off as we are ignited by the realization that the great God of heaven has given up everything in our behalf. The Gospel of Jesus Christ frees us from ourselves!

What all of us need is the will to look at others with respect. The cross tells us God loved us to the degree that God saw us as valued sons and daughters. God saw us from a Father's heart. God makes peace in our hearts in a way that allows us to become peacemakers in a world of tumult and godless uproar.

Almost everyone is in favor of peace; very few are peacemakers. The peacemaker is willing to do one of two things, and both are painful: to live with the uprooting that making authentic peace often requires, or to subjugate willingly one's own retaliatory instincts in order to establish an atmosphere where productive negotiating can emerge. There will, for instance, be no authentic spiritual peace in a person's heart until sin is dealt with. Sin must be uprooted and cast out. Christ bore that upheaval (and pain!). He gives us the grace to tolerate the pain of repentance. The lack of peace between two human beings sometimes is overcome only when both are willing to cool their retaliatory anger so that they are enabled to tolerate each other at a table of reconciliation. Often the most painful thing for us is to swallow is our pride. Again, Christ's forgiveness gives us the grace to tolerate the swallowing.

Does Christ come "to give peace" instead of "division"? Of course he does. But he didn't come leisurely walking among us with the gift of peace under his arm as a handout. The peace we needed had to be won. Thank God, a prince went forth for our sakes, the Prince of Peace, who now wants nothing more than that we, too, should be peacemakers across the earth.

Sabotaging
The Sabbath

Proper 16 *Luke 13:10-17*
Pentecost 14
Ordinary Time 21

We wish the story here would have ended another way. Yes, it was the sabbath (always meant to be a *beautiful* day for God's people!). And even on the sabbath people become sick or continue to be sick. Jesus notices a woman, all hunched over, obviously one who had been ill for a long time. He is a merciful Lord, so he takes the initiative to call her over and lay his hands on her. In these gracious acts, the woman is healed on the spot. Her body is straightened again, and she praises God for God's goodness.

From here on, I say, we wish the story would have ended another way. Wouldn't it have been nice if all the people standing around witnessing this touching scene could have joined the woman in praising God for God's goodness? Indeed, the whole idea of worshiping a loving God on the sabbath could have been thus reinforced in a powerful way.

But that is not what happened. As soon as Jesus finishes his lovely deed, the keepers of the sabbath, the religious leaders, become indignant. The ruler of the synagogue reminds everyone that there are six other days in the week when such deeds of healing could be done; even such a kind deed as healing was not allowable on the seventh day. Healing was considered work, and, as every good Jew knew (how could they forget it?), the sabbath means no work.

Jesus, of course, is stirred up by this heartless interpretation. He reminds the religious leaders of their double standard in this matter: how they regularly go about caring for their own animals on the sabbath by giving them water, but are seemingly unable to accept a similar propriety of caring for sick *human beings* on the sabbath. In the eyes of the crowd taking this all in, Jesus put the religious leaders to shame and gained the crowd's admiration for what he had done and said. A perfectly beautiful situation ends up in unpleasant tension. How sad.

All of this occurred because the religious leaders thought Jesus was somehow sabotaging the sabbath. And, in a way, Jesus was accusing *them* also of sabotaging the sabbath in an equally serious way. Let's see what we can learn from these conflicting viewpoints.

We can begin by pointing out that the ruler of the synagogue here should be encouraged for wanting to guard the sabbath. God gave the sabbath for salutary reasons. The rhythm of our lives and bodies calls for predictable periods of rest. We need a sabbath for the welfare of our own bodies and spirits. In addition, the sabbath affords a reasonable time for families to be together. God realizes that families need time for nurturing. The sabbath can also serve as a discipline that ensures an ongoing corporate worship among God's people. This religious leader saw the necessity of all these good things happening, so he rightly wanted to guard the sabbath from intrusions that might threaten its observance.

Good for him! Would that we in America, for instance, had a more clear-cut vision and practice concerning Sundays! We have not been able to successfully maintain Sunday as a sabbath in our country. Most commercial ventures are open for business, and one thing has led to another. Sundays are no longer sacred. The decline of Sunday worship in America seems to take place in direct correspondence to the increase of secular activities on Sundays. We might further inquire whether there isn't a relationship between the decline of family values and the decline of Sunday worship. We might even inquire whether our loss of well-being (health?) is caused by our refusal to give the body its deserved sabbath rest.

So, you see, we cannot fully dock the ruler of the synagogue in this story for trying to guard the observance of the sabbath day. He had good intentions.

What happened here is that good intentions were carried too far. In fact, they were carried so far that something altogether good and lovely became an ugly occasion. We can desire to guard a good thing so much that we suffocate the goodness of it in the process. So the religious leaders took God's masterful idea of the sabbath and pushed it too far. They pushed it so far that, believe it or not, it became acceptable to pass by the needs of another human being if it meant maintaining the authenticity of a certain day of the week.

How many times you and I end up doing something just as ridiculous! We carry our good intentions too far! We want our children to turn out "nice," so we over-discipline them to the extent that we sometimes profoundly injure their inner spirits and fill them with fear and distrust. We want our children to be "good students," but we burden them with so much study and homework that they never quite have time also to learn how to relate pleasingly to their peers; after all, "all work and no play makes Jack a dull boy." There are so many occasions in life when we want things "to turn out well." The trick is to refrain from forcing the issue to the extent that we end up with negative results.

There once was a loving couple who had the wife's elderly mother living with them. Their concern was for her security while both of them went away to work each day. They finally seemed satisfied after they had devised a system of twelve different locks and bolts for the front and back doors of the house! The only problem was that they overlooked the old woman's technical ability to operate all these devices. When a friend would want to call on her during the day, or when she would want to go out and enjoy the backyard, she had to turn down such opportunities because she didn't know how to get all the locks and bolts open! She ended up being a daytime prisoner, all in the name of feeling "secure." One doesn't even want to think of what might have happened if there had ever been a fire in the house. Her children had good intentions but carried them too far. The sabbath, too, needs to be guarded, but the religious leaders of Jesus' day carried things too far.

Then, secondly, we can notice in this story how a deed that is beautiful and good in itself can cause contention. Isn't it amazing that anyone would have complained about the helpful, graceful act Jesus did here? Think of it, this woman in the story had borne her infirmity for eighteen years. To have someone come along and relieve such a burden would have to be considered the most exquisite of human deeds.

But in this case, a perfectly good deed caused contention. In our own lives, we can have such an experience. There is, for instance, the proverbial mother of the bride, who takes a wonderfully fine day, such as her daughter's wedding, and turns it into a tension-filled day preceded by months of laborious planning and followed by months of regret and fatigue for everyone else in the family. Thank God that such Victorian concepts of executing everything "just right" have faded somewhat, so that most social occasions these days turn out to be what they were intended for — a good time of relaxation, fun, and pleasant conversation.

When you think of it, just about everything in life is supposed to be pleasant and enjoyable, and can be! But it seems like so much that was meant to be pleasant and enjoyable is marred by contention: our childhood, our school days, marriage, family life, our jobs and careers, and on and on. Likewise here, an act of kindness on the Lord's day ends in an uproar.

Things ended up the way they did (and do in our lives), because of someone's selfish spirit, in this case the spirit of jealousy. It is fairly obvious that this ruler of the synagogue had a concern beyond guarding the sabbath day from abuse. It is clear that he was jealous of Jesus. As the keeper of the synagogue, he felt that his own role as an enforcer of sabbath rules was being deliberately challenged or made light of. But surely Jesus was doing no more here than showing the typical human concern for which he was known. He wanted this woman to be relieved of her long burden — that was his only motive. But it was jealousy that turned his good deed into something questionable.

The synagogue ruler tried to camouflage his jealousy, as we all do. He purported to have the highest and holiest of motives: guarding the sanctity of God's sacred day. He probably even thought at first that no one would notice his real motives. He thought the crowd would support him. But jealousy is something difficult to hide. It usually sticks out everywhere; people notice our true motives more than we are ready to admit (and more than *they* are ready to admit, as well). People don't like to embarrass us; but they know.

The end doesn't always justify the means. Even if the ruler of the synagogue had the high motive of guarding the sabbath day from abuse, there was no excuse to pass by human need when it faced him. All of this is similar to the situation we find in the famous parable of Jesus called "The Good Samaritan." In that parable you recall how two other representatives of true religion passed by the bleeding victim lying in the ditch. It took a man who was not considered religious to bring aid finally in that case of obvious human need.

So Jesus was not about to allow love to be superseded by a religious demand that in itself was largely instructive. It was always love that informed Jesus; he was faithful to every call involving human need. Jesus would overthrow the strict demands of the law if it meant saving a lost soul.

This is the dynamic behind the whole story of our salvation, isn't it? Strictly speaking God was under no obligation to save you and me. In fact, the demands of God's law indicated that you and I should be condemned. But God did not come around reminding us, "You made your bed; now sleep in it." Maybe you have been in a gift shop or a pottery store where all kinds of fragile vases and plates were for sale. Perhaps you noticed a warning sign on the shelf in such places. It read, "You break it; you pay for it."

That was not God's attitude toward you and me, was it? Our sins stretch from *A* to *Z*. You and I have run the gamut of God's holy law, and we have broken it. Our sins from birth to the grave make us ten times more ill than the poor old woman in the story, whose back was hunched for eighteen years. As pride-filled sinners, we have gone around breaking God's holy law at will, and a lot of times we haven't even felt sorry about it.

What did God do in light of our sins? God didn't come back at us with the indictment, "You broke it; you pay for it." No, even though we didn't accidentally break the treasured gift of life but *willfully* dashed it to pieces, God has not thrown the book at us, demanding payment. God did not appeal to the fact that God's holy law is always and forever in effect. No, God allowed grace to hold sway; God allowed love to fulfill the law. God provided a way out.

The Bible tells us that "when the time had fully come, God sent forth his Son, born of woman, born *under the law*, to redeem those *who were under the law* ..." (Galatians 4:4-5). Christ bore the law for us. God's love saw our human need, and love led the way — all the way to his bitter death on the cross.

This story ends on a positive note: "... all the people rejoiced at all the glorious things that were done by him" (v. 17). Christ did a glorious deed here when he responded to human need by healing this woman, no matter what day of the week it was. Christ did an even more glorious deed when he mounted the cross to pay the price for our misdeeds. We will now gratefully gather on every sabbath to bring our thanksgiving in the Eucharist. And when we leave, we will feel nurtured and empowered to serve every human need around us! As we so serve one another, we will not be sabotaging the sabbath; we will be fulfilling it!

A Ministry
Of Hospitality

Proper 17 *Luke 14:1, 7-14*
Pentecost 15
Ordinary Time 22

Maybe you've heard the humorous story about the pastor who was having difficulty with his assigned parking space on the church parking lot. People parked in his spot whenever they pleased, even though there was a sign that clearly said, "This space reserved." He thought the sign needed to be more clear, so he had a different sign made, which read, "Reserved for Pastor Only." Still people ignored it and parked in his space whenever they felt like it. "Maybe the sign should be more forceful," he thought. So he devised a more intimidating one, which announced, "Thou shalt not park here." That sign didn't make any difference either. Finally, he hit upon the words that worked; in fact, nobody ever took his parking place again. The sign read, "The one who parks here preaches the sermon on Sunday morning!"

I tell you this story because most of you would probably hedge at the prospect of such a ministry: preaching the sermon on a Sunday morning. You would probably feel uncomfortable about doing that because of a lack of experience and training. But what, then, *is* your ministry? For you see, there are a variety of ministries in which *all* the people of a church can be involved. These ministries are based on various gifts we have as people. Saint Paul once made a list of these gifts when he talked about church people being involved in such things as preaching, teaching, administering, caretaking, praying, or even arbitrating.

The Gospel reading here, as well as the other two readings selected for this Sunday, set before us a vision of a common ministry that *all* of us can be a part of. I would call it something like "a ministry of hospitality."

Let's begin by looking at this concept of hospitality. All three Bible readings remind us not to set ourselves above other people. When we are together as the people of God, we ought to give place to one another. We ought to be *hospitable*. The reading from Proverbs says, "Do not exalt yourself ... do not claim a place...." In the Second Reading, the writer to the Hebrews encourages us, "Keep on loving each other as brothers. Do not forget to entertain strangers, for by so doing some people have entertained angels without knowing it." Finally, today's Gospel reading brings us the parable about the wedding guests. Jesus warns us that if you immediately claim a place of honor at such a gathering, you had better be prepared to experience some embarrassment when a more honored guest is ushered to your seat, and you are forced to take one of the undesirable spaces at the back of the hall. Then Jesus concludes by saying that if you want to be truly hospitable when you give a luncheon or dinner, you ought not invite your same old friends all the time but rather people who could never repay you, like the poor, the crippled, the lame, and the blind.

Jesus is beginning to build a case here for the truth that *there are no throwaways when it comes to human beings.* Everybody is worthy of your attention and greeting. There is no one who doesn't deserve your hospitality and mine. In fact, Jesus suggests that you are taking a real chance when you slight certain people; you see, they might just turn out to be angels you did not know about!

On the surface, this is a story about good social manners at a wedding. But its deeper purpose is to remind you and me in the family of God about our calling to be genuinely hospitable to one another. In the background looms the even brighter message about God's hospitality to each and every one of us (sinners that we are!), a hospitality which God showed us in the ministry of God's own blessed son, our Lord Jesus Christ. So, what is this ministry of hospitality?

To help us, let's look more closely at this word "hospitality." Before we look at its literal meaning, we need to point out that there is a difference between hospitality and entertaining. A psychologist put it this way:

> *Hospitality must not be confused with entertaining ... Entertaining says, "Come to my house; admire my possessions; see the beautiful way the table is laid. Enjoy the scrumptious food that has taken me all week to prepare. See how perfectly neat and tidy and clean my house is. Come and listen to my views and thoughts."*
>
> *Entertaining is hard, stressful, because through it we perpetuate the myth that we are perfect. We put up a facade saying that we manage our lives perfectly and that our children are perfectly disciplined and obedient.*
>
> *Hospitality is totally different. We do not seek to portray a "perfect" image; people can love us in our weakness, relax with us, and enjoy our company.*

An even deeper meaning of the word "hospitality" emerges when we realize that this word comes from the same source as two similar sounding words, "hospice" and "hospital." The word "hospice" means "shelter" and the word "hospital" means "a place of healing." In this light, we can examine some of our own words and actions toward other people. Do my words and actions provide a *shelter* for other persons when they are around me? Or, do my words and deeds promote a sense of *healing* for other people when they are around me? How *hospitable* am I, really?

For a moment, let us push the word "hospice" to its limits. We are aware that today the word "hospice" usually refers to a special kind of care or place meant for people who are *dying*. People with terminal illnesses receive hospice care.

In the church we need to remember, as we deal with one another — with fellow church members, with visitors, with other folks from the community — that there may be among us those who are *dying*! They are dying on the inside; for whatever reason, life is currently treating them harshly and they feel broken. Some are dying just to know someone; they have few, if any, friends. Some are dying to feel connected; they don't feel like they belong to the human race anymore. Some are dying to be affirmed; they are weary from feeling that they amount to nothing. Some are dying to be touched, even if only by eye contact, or by some word of acknowledgment from another human being. All these people need *hospice* care; they need the hospitality of the church, because inwardly they are dying. They need a place of shelter, no matter how fleeting, where they can catch another breath of air to sustain them, lest they die.

There was a minister who had a favorite slogan that he often repeated in his sermons. He said, "The church is not like a country club; it's more like a hospital." That's what Jesus was saying here when he gave us the direction, "... do not invite your friends ... or your rich neighbors ... invite the poor, the crippled, the lame, and the blind...." You and I are not in the church to impress one another or to win power struggles; we are here to minister to one another in our weaknesses. We are here to be *hospitable*.

Now nobody can specifically tell you what your ministry of hospitality should consist of; we should never over-define such a highly personal ministry. But we must — each of us — define that ministry for ourselves.

To encourage us about this, let's look at the ministry of Jesus. In a way, we could call Christ's ministry to you and me a ministry of hospitality. Yes, that is what he showed us. The apostle Paul stated it in that singular sentence, "While we were yet sinners Christ died for us" (Romans 5:8). Think of it, "yet sinners...." God did not withhold hospitality from us until we straightened ourselves out. While we were sinners, Christ was hospitable toward us by going to the cross and dying for us, in our place. Noticing our sin, Christ did not refuse to acknowledge us. He did not stop talking to us. He did not withhold information from us about God's love. No, in Christ, God made eye contact with us. The Word became flesh. The face of God now faced us. Looking into that face we felt sheltered and healed. Looking at his cross we know we *are* healed — cleansed and forgiven in the blood of Jesus

Christ. The cross enables us to follow the divine model of hospitality.

Again the apostle Paul encourages us toward such Christly hospitality when he writes to the Philippian Christians in chapter two of his letter, "Let this mind be in you that was in Christ Jesus ... who humbled himself and took on the form of a servant and ... became obedient unto death, even death on a cross." In this great passage, Paul reminds us how Jesus fulfilled the lesson of the parable we are considering in this Gospel reading. Christ, who is the first, became the last, so that we, the last, might be first, having all our sins washed away by his obedience at the cross.

So now, empowered by the cross of Christ, we each have our own ministry of hospitality. This ministry is more than showing good manners in public. It is a *redemptive* ministry, like Christ's, whereby we bring a sense of healing and genuine acceptance to all other people.

And we should get specific about our own ministry of hospitality. Perhaps, for instance, you have the gift of gab — the ability to talk at ease with just about anyone. You could be an effective greeter to the strangers who visit your church. You could be that little spark of light to many longtime members of the parish to whom no one else seems to speak or give notice.

On the other side of the coin, you can be one of those church members who responds in a vital way when others greet you. Someone else takes the initiative and shows enough of a caring spirit to say "Good morning" to you, but sometimes all that can be observed in response is a faint grunt of acknowledgment or a slight tip of the head.

But out of this initial hospitality shown one another in the church hallways needs to blossom a deeper hospitality whereby people come to know that God loves them and cares for them, too. In this regard Christian hospitality always finally needs to involve some word of witness to God's love in Christ. This is another way of saying that Christian hospitality ultimately involves *evangelism*: speaking God's good word of love to another human soul. What could be more hospitable? How could we provide more of a sheltering spirit or speak a more healing word than to remind someone of the love of God in the cross of Jesus Christ? With this singular message on the lips of its members, the church does indeed rise above mere country club status and reveals itself as the glorious household of faith. As the old hymn puts it, "If you cannot speak like angels, if you cannot preach like Paul, you can tell the love of Jesus, you can say he died for all." God bless your ministry — your ministry of hospitality!

The Crux Of
Being A Christian

Proper 18   *Luke 14:25-33*
Pentecost 16
Ordinary Time 23

For a moment, call to mind Psalm 23. The Lord is my shepherd. Green pastures. Still waters. A cup overflowing. Oh, yes! There is a serene side of being a Christian.

But this Gospel reading in Luke crashes in on our spiritual serenity. The spell of a peaceful religion is shattered. We become startled as we hear Jesus speak these uprooting words. Some believers have admitted to being shocked and puzzled by what Jesus says here. How about you? How do these words strike you?

> *If anyone comes to me and does not hate his own father and mother and wife and children and brothers and sisters, yes, and even his own life, he cannot be my disciple.*
> — Luke 14:26

These words bring us forthrightly to what we might call the crux of being a Christian. You have heard of the word "crux." In English we commonly use it in the little phrase, "the crux of the matter." By that phrase we usually are referring to the heart of the matter, to the thing that brings us to the distinguishing feature about something, to that which reveals the core of the matter. It is interesting and telling that this word "crux" is letter for letter the same word as the Latin word *crux*. In Latin the word means "cross."

So, when we talk about the crux of being a Christian, we're not only talking about the heart of the matter, but, by using the word "crux" we are automatically saying that this heart of the matter of being a Christian involves something of the cross, something of feeling crucified, something that strongly suggests a painful side. This is not to say that all of Christianity is painful, but it *is* to say that the distinguishing feature of being a Christian will involve a painful side, for surely the crux — the cross — involves sacrifice, pain, and even death.

So what is this painful thing, this crux about which Jesus speaks here? What is it for which Jesus shockingly announces we should be willing to hate father and mother, spouse, children, and all the rest of the family? What is it for which we must be willing to give up everything? What is the thing about which, as Jesus puts it, we should "count the cost"?

At first we are probably tempted to think that it is something like "our salvation" or "our faith in Christ." But, you see, upon closer analysis we would have to admit that everything concerning our salvation and our faith involves no cost, no pain, no crux whatsoever on *our* part. Good Christian doctrine teaches us that Christ bore *all* the pain, all the cost, all the cross. Christ alone saves us, Christians preach, and even our faith in him is totally God's gift to us.

So we are still left with the question about what the crux of being a Christian is. Throughout this reading, however, Jesus never tells us specifically what the crux is. But I believe that today's second Bible reading *does* reveal this crux of the matter to us. That's probably exactly why this reading is coupled with today's Gospel reading, so let's look at that second reading now.

It's an unusual reading because, you see, the book of Philemon consists of only one chapter, so that the reading consists of this entire chapter, save the last two verses. In the touching story it tells, we have a wonderful illustration about what the crux of being a Christian is.

What is that story? Briefly, it involves three characters: the apostle Paul, his friend named Philemon, and a servant who worked in Philemon's house with the interesting name, Onesimus.

Now this servant Onesimus was really less than a servant; he was a slave in Philemon's household. Despite the fact that Philemon was a Christian, he continued the Roman practice of having slaves in his household. Throughout the Roman empire there were millions of such slaves. They were totally at their masters' mercy.

It seems that Onesimus was accused of stealing something valuable from Philemon's house. Fearing the consequences, Onesimus ran away. Lo and behold, he ends up in the great city of Rome; somehow he became acquainted there with the apostle Paul, who was serving a sentence in the Roman prison. Being the missionary he was, Paul converted Onesimus to the Christian faith. But Paul realized that he couldn't keep Onesimus under his wing indefinitely. So he convinces Onesimus that the wisest course for him would be to return to his former master, Philemon. But to soften the blow, Paul writes a letter to Philemon, exhorting him to receive his runaway slave, Onesimus, with forgiveness and love. After all, Paul reminds him, Onesimus is now a Christian and should be viewed by Philemon as a new brother in the faith. Paul puts punch behind his request by offering to replace anything Onesimus might have stolen. How could Philemon refuse to receive lovingly his former slave after an appeal like that from none other than the apostle Paul? We assume that Onesimus returned to Philemon and in some respect lived happily ever after. So far the story.

This story, I submit, reveals to us what is the crux of being a Christian. It all has to do with what Philemon here finally determined to do: to reach out a hand of acceptance and forgiveness to someone who had sinned against him, even when, technically speaking (that is, in the eyes of others), he wouldn't have to. This was a *painful* decision, a decision involving something of the cross, no doubt, since, in his heart, Philemon was probably crying out to Onesimus, "I'll get you for this!" Here is the Christian call of accepting other persons, not because they deserve it, but because we realize Christ died on the cross for them, too. It's the ultimate call of swallowing our own pride. We all know how painful that can be. The story of Philemon is reminiscent of the words of Jesus: "Love your enemies ... turn the other cheek ... if your brother offends you, go to him and work it out." To carry out these words means *pain* for most of us.

So it is that Jesus warns in the Gospel reading, "... sit down and count the cost...." Yes, this kind of discipleship may indeed involve renouncing everything: your very *self.* Jesus, of course, is himself the perfect example of the very thing he calls us to do. Look at his crux, that is, the climactic moment when he hung upon the cross. He was suffering in physical pain there, yes. But the greater pain may have been mustering the last ounce of love whereby he was able to bless his executioners and say, "Father, forgive them, for they know not what they are doing."

This reminds me of a similar story, Christ-like in nature, that transpired in the Chicago area a few years back. At that time a young man had publicly accused Cardinal Bernardin of the Chicago archdiocese of misconduct in office. The charges were ravaging and destructive. As it turned out, the tables were turned; the young man withdrew his charges, admitting they were totally false. Several months later the young man was on his own deathbed, dying from a fatal illness. It must have been with some considerable pain that Cardinal Bernardin then went to this young man and blessed him, wishing him the eternal peace of Christ. There is a high cost to such faithful discipleship. Can we call it "the pain of forgiving"?

Lest we too quickly agree with all of this, let us remind ourselves that our capacity for holding grudges and nursing personal hatreds is an awesome force to overcome. We are all sinners, and that means we are held in the clutches of sin. Much of our sin takes place within the setting of human relationships. In our dealings with other people we find it difficult to practice understanding and love and forgiveness. The devil pushes us toward estrangement and brokenness and icy silence; he champions the loss of eye contact between people who ought to be looking one another straight in the eye. Satan convinces us never to suffer the painful humiliation of giving in; he always presses us toward maintaining our own selfish stance. "Rights rather than relationships" is the devil's theme. Environmentally and socially speaking, our world stands at the precipice of destruction because some people stubbornly insist upon their rights, not caring what is destroyed in the process.

In contrast, the mind of Philemon is to suppress, painfully, if need be, any rightful behavior and to surprise others with the hand of fellowship. But again, don't always expect others to encourage such a stance. Do you remember the time when Jesus was talking with his disciples about going to Jerusalem to suffer and be killed, and on the third day be raised? Peter grabbed Jesus, took him aside and rebuked him, we are told, saying, "God forbid, Lord! This shall never happen to you." But then Jesus turned to Peter and said, "Get behind me, Satan! You are a hindrance to me; for you are not on the side of God, but of men" (Matthew 16:21-23). Those who choose the path of redemptive suffering can expect criticism from even their closest friends. It is evident that the friendship between Peter and Jesus was strained at that moment. Sometimes loyalty to God must transcend maintaining smooth human relationships.

It is in this light that we can now perhaps understand what Jesus was saying in the opening verses of this Gospel reading. Remember the shocking words: "If anyone comes to me and does not hate his own father and mother and wife and children and brothers and sisters, yes, even his own life, he cannot be my disciple." Understandably it can be those who love us most — father and mother, and all the rest of the family — who jump when our "rights" are threatened, or when injustice is threatening our well-being, and stick up for us. Like Jesus did to Peter, we might at that point have to turn our backs on the people who love us most and whom we love most, for the sake of being faithful to God's mission. While our parents are shouting, "No one's gonna push *my* kid around!" we may have to follow through and demonstrate a higher wisdom and a more profound love — an undeserved love, a grace so unexpected that it is amazing, indeed. This is what Jesus did when he died on the cross.

Because Jesus did that for us, we will live in forgiveness with all other people, even though they may not deserve it, and even when, in the eyes of most others, we could rightfully withhold forgiveness. This is the crux of being a Christian. God help you carry such a cross!

God's Passionate Concern

Proper 19 *Luke 15:1-10*
Pentecost 17
Ordinary Time 24

The two parables that Jesus tells here each involve a single character possessed by a passionate concern. In the first, a shepherd who tends a flock of one hundred sheep discovers that one of them is lost. His passionate concern is to find that single lost one. In the second parable, a woman who has ten silver coins loses one of them. Her passionate concern is to find that single lost one.

In the two opening verses of this story Luke tells us how it came about that Jesus told these parables. The Pharisees and the scribes were murmuring among themselves about how the tax collectors and sinners always seemed to hover around Jesus, listening to him. The disturbing feature seemed to be that Jesus not only encouraged this alliance; he even deliberately returned the favor by sitting down and eating with them. Sinners were drawn to Jesus, and he seemed drawn to them! Those lost souls seemed to be a passionate concern of his. Jesus noticed the disapproving attitude of the church leaders. To explain his actions he told the two parables.

They reveal three marvelous truths about God.

1. God the creator does not leave God's creatures to fend for themselves; God is like a shepherd who constantly broods over

them; God is like an old woman who keeps track of her treasure and notices when a single coin is missing.

2. God wants to *reclaim* what is lost; God has a passionate concern about this.

3. A great *joy* is felt when what has been lost is found and restored.

For a time now, let us revel in these marvelous truths about God, for they are truths, finally, that involve every last one of us.

These three truths, in a way, tell us what God is like. That's always a question of the times, isn't it? What God is like is a proposition we humans have always been devoted to, and the present time is no different. Who is God? What is God like?

In many respects our answers have reflected a serious poverty of thought. In fact, our answers often have been poor because they have hardly been answers at all. They reek of imprecision. They are so general as to be mostly useless. Think of it, grown men and women mumbling about "a Man Upstairs" when talking about God. Or how about parents, seeking to comfort (or warn?) their children about God by reminding them that "Someone up there is watching you." In the worst instances we have forsaken any direct reference to God and instead talk about him in code language with phrases like "family values" or "moral precepts." Others talk about people having "a religious side that they never show," because they have no idea about who God is or what God is like. The prevalence of such generic forms of God is a fact of the times. One would be hard-pressed to find out what God is like by listening to the talk of many folks today.

But here in these two parables Jesus gives us a dynamic and precise reading about what God is like. God is like a shepherd, totally involved with God's flock; God is not some distant caretaker. When even one among so many sheep becomes lost, this shepherd springs into action for the sake of finding and rescuing that precious one. When he does find the lost one, he doesn't kick it in the side and start hollering at it. With joyful satisfaction the shepherd places the lost one on his shoulders and rushes back home to tell his friends the good news.

In the same spirit, a woman with silver coins values each one for what it is worth, so that when even one is lost, she will turn the house upside down until she finds it, smiling with delight when she does.

This then is what God is like. God is in the midst of God's people, always caring for them. God has a passionate concern for any one of them that happens to become lost. In God's eyes no human being ever gets lost in the crowd.

Indeed lost souls must be found. There must be someone on the outside of the situation who has a sufficient concern to take action. The action itself must be "passionate," intense, and disruptive, if need be, like the woman who "lights a lamp and sweeps the house and seeks diligently until she finds [the coin]" (v. 8). Holy commotion is the only acceptable response in such a radical situation! You and I are not only sinners; we are lost souls.

Understanding this, a reader can correspondingly understand the life and ministry of Jesus Christ as it is portrayed in the New Testament. We have to remove the glowing lenses of religiosity (or of idealistic childhood) that have overlaid a sweet harmlessness on the life of Jesus. A careful look at the New Testament pages reveals a sharply-etched Christ who frequently sets polite people on edge, because, after all, this Son of God is on a *search*. Jesus would not hesitate to sweep aside dusty truths and practices if they kept him from finding lost people and ministering to them. He would turn the house of Israel upside down, if need be, to find the lost and rescue them.

In this mission Christ would exhibit an ambiguous outlook. In one sense he was a minister to the masses. He appealed to the crowds. He involved them in his ministry by the thousands. But he was essentially a missionary to the individual. His telephoto-type vision ultimately gave way to a zoom lens-type focus on the one lost soul. While the crowds during his ministry became larger and larger, Satan never was able to trick him into believing that bigger is better. Finally, each soul must be uncovered, each person retrieved, each heart forgiven. The Christ of the Gospels is like the shepherd who will "leave the ninety-nine in the wilderness, and go after the one which is lost, until he finds it" (v. 4).

So this brings us to the lost — who they are and how they got that way. We are talking here, of course, about you and me and about every human being there ever was. Are you ready? Are you up to being called "a lost soul"? I don't think most of us are. The stories about us are perennial. We pack up the family and are off to strange places on our summer vacation. We travel down the freeways and interstates with no trouble. But when we make an exit for the purpose of zeroing in on our destination, we find that the actual lay of the land is slightly more complicated than what the map showed when we read it at home. After some aimless driving, we sense that we have lost our direction and don't know quite where we are. But the fact of being lost is hard to admit, it seems. We refuse to get out the map and study it again. We will not humiliate ourselves by stopping at a farmhouse to ask for directions. In fact, we will try to bluff our way with all the others in the car, until even one of the youngest in the back seat catches on and asks, "Dad, are we lost?"

Most of us try to carry on and pretend we didn't hear that question. We find it very difficult indeed to admit that we are lost. And the term "lost soul" sends us into total repugnancy. Actually, most of us would probably prefer being referred to as a sinner. At least it sounds adult-like in comparison to being considered lost, like some child. The idea of being a sinner might even stir up a kind of twisted admiration from others, while being considered lost could only lead to pity.

It is a pity, however, because the lost are powerless. Unless there is intervention, they are beyond hope. Like lost sheep, they are totally out of their element; like lost coins, they can only lie there motionless. The lost are always hopelessly lost, as the apostle Paul assessed the situation when he said, "... you were *dead* in trespasses and sin ..." (Ephesians 2:1). It is useless to imagine that such souls can "find themselves" again!

So God's concern to find us *is* so passionate precisely because we are so lost — totally lost, beyond finding ourselves. Passionate to the point of enduring exactly what that Latin word means: suffering. Oh, yes, our shepherd was willing to endure the suffering — the passion — of the cross, if that is what it would take to restore us, to reclaim us, to find us in the sense of bringing us back home to the safety of the sheepfold. Jesus Christ did for us what no one else could do. Only he is the shepherd; only he could find us. "This man receives sinners and eats with them," complained the religious leaders. And we might add that besides receiving sinners and eating with them, Christ *dies* for them. In his own body he bears the pain of their waywardness, of their sins. It is in the web and maze of sin's entangling forces where the shepherd plucks the lost one from certain destruction. In that coagulation of sin's suffocating strands, the divine eye of the Savior discerns the lost wanderer and restores the soul, returning it to green pastures beside still waters. In passion and suffering the shepherd accomplishes all of this for a single lost one, for *you* and *me*.

Thus it is that passionate concern gives way to unrestrained joy. When the shepherd finds the lost one, he lays it on his shoulders rejoicing, and he invites friends and neighbors into his circle of celebration. When the woman has found the lost coin, she calls together her friends and neighbors to share her unbounded joy. After God finds us, God does not punish us; God puts us on God's shoulder, parading us home in honor, with a smile on God's face that brings a smile to our own.

For a few years now I have been hearing reports on television about a particular movement in Christianity where the chief feature of its public worship involves smiling to the point of belly-laughing. The worship leader leads in the laughing, and before you know it, the whole congregation is more or less laughing their heads off. It causes a smile just to think about it, and I guess it is that dynamic that is operative in such church services — one laugh leads to another.

Should we all try it right now? Maybe if we did, we'd all be so shocked by the uncontrollable joy, that, with embarrassment, we'd consider the whole situation less than respectful. But wouldn't you admit that within the Church of Jesus Christ there needs to be a clearer witness to the fact that God is happy to have found you and me, wayward sinners that we are? Isn't there indeed a place at which we ought to be listening for this divine laughter as it exults over an entire congregation that knows salvation and rescue through Jesus Christ?

And then how fine it would be to experience that divine laughter catching on among us in the congregation of God! The father of the prodigal son had the right idea. When he saw his son coming down the road, a smile streaked across his face and he didn't stop smiling for a long time. In short order, this father stages a party for his lost son, a celebration for one who was back home again. All that kind of joy needs to become a characteristic of our Christian gatherings, an observable tone that others don't have to strain to uncover when they are among the family of faith.

Sometimes we are unduly reserved in the church because, despite our salvation, we are so aware of the great cost of that salvation. It's almost as though once we know the horrible cost that God expended for our rescue it would never again seem quite proper to smile and laugh in God's presence. Must we not at such a point be very careful not to make such spiritual frowning a kind of test for the genuineness of faith? And would not such a test then become a kind of work or accomplishment that we add to the saving work of Christ? Somber churches and somber church gatherings almost suggest that somehow our salvation has not yet been settled, as though there is something yet to be suffered. Churches of laughter and joy, on the other hand, more properly suggest that all has been accomplished, salvation is complete, there is nothing more to do but rejoice and be glad in the Good News. Such is the gift, such is the amazing grace, such is the total joy of the Christian gospel! God's passionate concern *now* is that each of us *enjoy* this salvation.

Clever Christians

Proper 20 *Luke 16:1-13*
Pentecost 18
Ordinary Time 25

There is nothing unusual in talking about faithful Christians, active Christians, committed Christians, obedient and humble Christians, about Christians who are loving and loyal. But *clever* Christians? Some of us may never have heard it put that way.

This is what surprises us about the parable here in Luke 16. Toward the end of it Jesus says that the "sons of light" (v. 8), that is, the people of God, ought to be clever in their religion, like the "sons of this world" are in their business dealings; the Christian enterprise calls for shrewdness! Let's try to understand a little more clearly what Jesus means by all of this as we consider the theme, "Clever Christians."

At first reading the whole story here may impress us as a little shocking, because it almost sounds like Jesus is using a criminal as an example of the type of person Christians should be. Look at the parable. There is this rich man, probably a successful farmer. He was so successful that he could afford to be an absentee landlord. He hired a manager to run the farm and keep the books. The manager in turn hired workers to do the actual farming. Most of the crops the workers raised were given back to the owner of the land as rent. The workers kept a small portion and that was the way they made a living. One day the rich owner got wind of a rumor that his hired manager was embezzling some of the funds, or at least wasn't running the business very efficiently. The owner called in the manager, told him he was fired, and that he should have his desk cleared and be out of the office by noon on Friday.

The manager took his boss seriously; he took his own shaky situation even more seriously. He immediately began wondering how he could save his own neck. He would be unemployed by noon on Friday — out on the street, humiliated, finished! All this demanded some quick and resourceful action. "Friends! — That's what I need, plenty of friends who will feel they owe me a favor when they see me down and out." Within seconds the whole plan flashes before him. He determines that he is not going to end up digging ditches or begging on street corners. He will go to all those who are working the farm and ask each of them the amount of their debt to the owner. Whatever it is, he will alter their bills so that they will only owe half as much, or two-thirds as much. At any rate each worker will receive a huge discount, thanks to the manager. What a way to build instant friendships! Very clever, indeed.

When the manager finishes clearing his desk, he is about to walk out into the Friday afternoon sunshine. His wealthy boss stops him for a parting shot. "You know, you were a lousy manager; but I have to hand it to you: your little farewell discounts to the workers were a shrewd stroke. You *are* a clever one, aren't you?"

At this point Jesus ends the story and tells his hearers, in effect, how wonderful it would be if the people of God could be that clever when it came to their religion. Typically, Jesus doesn't say exactly what he means by being "clever" in the practice of religion, but surely he must have meant something like the following.

First of all, didn't he mean that we should be clever enough to face the facts when they are staring us in the face? When the boss told the manager he was fired, he believed him. The manager didn't engage in any denial about the seriousness of his situation. He didn't say, "Oh, my boss wouldn't do that to *me*; why I've been with him for over twenty years. He'll cool down in a couple of hours when he realizes what a valued employee I really am!" Nor did the manager assume that all of this was not as serious as it sounded, as though, after all, he was an experienced worker and could get another job in a snap.

No, we do not hear that kind of talk at all. Immediately he asked himself, "What shall I *do*...?" He committed himself to immediate action. He shifted gears instantly until his thinking was open only to the most clever and most resourceful thoughts.

When it comes to getting serious about religion, do not a lot of people surmise that they have plenty of time? This is true of unbelievers and believers alike. The unbeliever concludes that religion, yes, is a nice twist in our cultural expression as human beings. A significant number of people seem to be taken by religion; it is part of their daily lives and even seems to be personally helpful or, at least for many, has a calming effect. Later on, when perhaps much of their lives are over and they have nothing else to do, then they too will try to find something meaningful in the Bible or in a church.

People who consider themselves believers also think along such lines at times. They are members of churches, or at least know they have been baptized or maybe even confirmed, but they never go to church. A lot of their relatives are active in the church, and here and there, at work or in school or among neighbors, they hear certain folks talking about going to church or being involved in some church activity. They consider themselves religious — even Christian — but they regard most of it as being something for a few who are attracted by "that sort of thing."

There are still other types of believers who *are* active in the church in the sense that they frequently attend services but otherwise practice a fairly "private religion," assuming that, after all, religion, like politics, is a private matter. They are in favor of something but never engaged in it, really.

There are yet other believers who go to church and are considered very active in church programs but who have concluded that they could never seriously adopt the teachings or moral standards of Christianity in certain portions of their everyday lives. Countless numbers of Christian young people may therefore be admirable church members, but they know that they will never say "no" to certain beckoning sexual partners until later in life when their passions cool down. Countless numbers of Christian business people may be pillars of the church, but they know that making a living *now* unfortunately involves ongoing indiscretions on their part.

You get the idea: unbelievers as well as believers go on and on, year after year, telling themselves that one day they are "going to do something" about this matter of religion, about this matter of doing God's will. Someday, the unbeliever surmises, I am going to get serious about the whole matter of religion. I am going to look into it. Some believers, the ones who never go to church, tell themselves deep down that they will try to find time to worship at some future date. Other believers, who only attend church, or still others, who are, as we said, pillars of the church, resolve that they will get down to the serious side of faith someday — the side that brings them to a personal and touching confrontation with the Lord Jesus Christ and to the moral heroism they know is part and parcel of rising above a merely hypocritical faith. All of these people know in their hearts that, as Jesus says here, "no servant can serve two masters," that "you cannot serve God and mammon." All of them know that there must come a day when Christ is either Lord or he is not Lord, when Christ *is* served or he is *not* served.

This "day that must come," frankly, is always today — now. It is this fact that this parable is all about. Clever Christians know that now is the time for action, for doing, not the time for denial about the crucialness of the situation. Clever Christians know that not to choose is to choose; that the apostle Paul was right when he said, "Now is the day of salvation."

With the Second World War behind him, the German Lutheran pastor, Martin Niemoeller, wrote his now famous confession called "I Didn't Speak Up," and it is apropos:

> *In Germany, the Nazis first came for the Communists, and I didn't speak up because I wasn't a Communist. Then they came for the Jews, and I didn't speak up because I wasn't a Jew. Then they came for the trade unionists, and I didn't speak up because I wasn't a trade unionist.*

Then they came for the Catholics, but I didn't speak up because I was a Protestant. Then they came for me, and by that time there was no one left to speak for me.

Would that all of those involved in the religious enterprise were as clever as the manager in this parable! "What shall I *do*...?" he immediately wondered. He quickly cleared his brain to answer that one. He did not deny the reality of his need to take action.

But this parable suggests being "clever Christians" involves something more. The manager here exercised sheer business shrewdness; Jesus is suggesting that in the area of religion the people of God should show a similar cleverness. They should not engage in shady practices or dishonesty, of course; nor should they function in the church for profit motives or selfish gain. But they should be committed to the kind of resourcefulness often employed in business circles for profit and gain.

Lest we think this observation of Jesus is outdated, it should be noted that many quarters of the Church are debating this very issue about being resourceful at the present time. Sometimes the issue is stated in questions like this: Should the churches as a *first* consideration devise forms and formats of worship that are "attractive" to people, or should such a "user-friendly" attitude be of secondary importance? Or how about moral issues? Do technology and other advancements of the twentieth century suggest a change in some of our moral stances, or does everything remain rigidly standard according to religious laws, some of which, by the way, are now over 4,000 years old?

The final answers to such questions are beyond the scope of a Sunday morning sermon, of course. But the very fact that such questions are being asked is an indication that churches are struggling with the issue of "cleverness" as it was brought up by Jesus in this parable. One fact is sure: most churches *have* adopted some of the ways of the world (of the business world, for instance) for the sake of effectively preaching the gospel. So, for instance, our church buildings use modern, thermostat-controlled heating and air-conditioning. Pastors think nothing of driving around in fully-equipped automobiles as they carry out their ministerial duties.

Church offices make widespread use of computers, printing equipment, and advertising expertise in communicating with parish and non-parish persons. The list could go on enumerating "clever" ways and methods commonly employed in churches concerned about effectively carrying on the mission of the Savior.

But more than anything, Jesus Christ is calling us in the Church to be resourceful in our mission because most of the world has not yet heard the saving gospel. Most have never heard God's saving verdict that could transform their lives and give them hope again. The majority of people in the world do not even know the name of Jesus Christ.

Like the manager in the parable, we need to be astute enough to recognize this as a radically serious terminal situation about which action is required forthwith. Then we need to take action — the cleverest and most effective kind available — so that millions more may come to know and believe the saving grace of the cross and resurrection of Jesus Christ.

But those resourceful ideas for our mission enterprise will probably fall into place if we have enough of a passion for human souls. It is the old story of valuing another person so highly that you want them to have the same eternal hope you do. Many years ago, probably fifty or more, there was a minister who published a book encouraging other ministers in their mission of bringing more people to Christ. The book was called *The Romance of Door Bells*. The author was trying to convince ministers that calling on people door-to-door by ringing their doorbells was one effective way of beginning the process of sharing the gospel with them. Today, with a lot of security and schedule concerns such door-to-door calling might not be the best way for most ministers to spend their time. But I do like the title of the book, *The Romance of Door Bells*, with its inherent reference about becoming involved with individual persons, one by one, and the assumption that this mission activity ought to be a romance — something we want to do because we love people, we are passionate about their welfare, and we have a heart for their future.

So let's do it: ring doorbells, use computers, change our ways, use ways old and new, and be watchful enough that we never miss a chance to proclaim to others the hope that is in us in Jesus Christ our Lord.

Finally, to encourage you and me about all of this, we can do no better than to take note of the resourcefulness God exercised in bringing you and me salvation. It was not too long after that fateful fall in the garden when God asked in effect, "What shall I do...?" Like a wise manager, God immediately committed to action. The serpent was promised, "I will put enmity between you and the woman, and between your seed and her seed; he shall bruise your head, and you shall bruise his heel" (Genesis 3:15). In that promise God decided that God would forthwith carry out a plan of salvation that would restore eternal life to God's children. How would God do that?

God reached way down into God's bag of resources, and concluded that God would send *himself* to us in such a winning way that we would believe in and trust God again. God would send God's very own son!

So in the quiet of an ancient midnight hour the little one was born and laid in a manger. Human features just like ours — the skin and fingernails, the gentle limbs and a baby's cry. How divinely clever that God should gift us with himself by sending us someone exactly like ourselves — the Lord Jesus Christ! Talk about resources: on Good Friday Christ steeled himself until he had rallied all of God's love and forgiveness in his own body, which he then forthrightly offered upon the cross for our sake. On the cross, all of God was given for all of us, because here finally was the only one who "was faithful in a little and faithful in much" (v. 10). Here finally, in God's own son, was one to whom God could entrust *everything*. Christ could not serve two masters, but only one. Christ *did not* serve two masters, but only one — and we are saved!

Surely God will give us the resources and the commitment to proclaim this saving word.

Keep Things Flowing

Proper 21 *Luke 16:19-31*
Pentecost 19
Ordinary Time 26

There was a beautiful lake that lost its zesty freshness. The water formerly had been clear. It was alluring to animals and people alike. But it became covered with a green scum. The farm animals became ill from drinking the water. Finally someone came by the lake who understood the problem. Debris collecting from the hard spring rains had stopped up the dam and prevented the free flow of water, not into the lake, but out of the lake. The spillway was cleared, and soon the lake was fresh and clean again. The flow *in and out* was necessary to keep the water pure!

Doesn't the same principle apply to you and me as human beings? The blessings of life flow *to* you and me, but we fail to realize that most of these blessings are not meant just to flow *to* us, but *through* us, for the good of others around us, especially for those in need.

In this Gospel reading we have one of those sad stories — even a somber story — about a person who didn't keep things flowing in his life, with the result that his life became clogged and ended in tragedy.

We don't know the man's name as Jesus told this story. Jesus simply called him "the rich man." We may take that to mean that the man was richly blessed. A lot of life's blessings had flowed *to* this man. But it seems that very few of those blessings flowed *through* him, reaching other people.

Jesus gives us this sparse description, "There was once a rich man who dressed in the most expensive clothes and lived in great luxury every day" (v. 19). Jesus doesn't say he was happy because he "dressed in the most expensive clothes." He doesn't say the man was joyful because "he lived in great luxury every day." Jesus simply says that a lot of life's blessings flowed into this man's life. Hardly anything, it seems, flowed through the man — to other people.

In fact Jesus makes it clear that most of the man's blessings got clogged in his own hand and rarely flowed through his life to others, except by accident. Jesus describes it: "There was also a poor man, named Lazarus, covered with sores, who used to be brought to the rich man's door, hoping to eat the bits of food that fell from the rich man's table" (vv. 20-21).

Surely part of the reason Jesus tells this story is to appeal to us to keep things flowing in our lives. Today Christ wants every Christian to pray, "Lord, as your blessings flow to me, may they continue to flow *through* me, for the good and encouragement of others!"

Life in general suggests *flowing* rather than stagnation. We want the blood and air to travel through our bodies; we try to avoid those things that cause a buildup of plaque and clogged arteries. In recent times we've come to appreciate the cycling and recycling that go on in nature. There seems to be a constant flow, the flow of life that cleanses, enriches and makes things new. The leaves of autumn will gradually flow into the soil of a future springtime. We are learning that unless our throwaway society begins to effectively recycle what it discards, we will clog the flow of our waters and atmosphere until we're literally choked to death.

You and I don't have to be financially rich people to apply the force of what Jesus is saying in this story. There are many levels and dimensions of life at which you and I have been greatly blessed. Many blessings have come *to us*; they are meant in large measure to travel *through* us to others.

Take the primary matter of our own faith and trust in Jesus Christ as our Lord and Savior. This is the greatest blessing we have! We know of salvation in Jesus Christ and we believe it. Think of it: In his mercy and love God has chosen us to be God's own. God's Son has died upon the cross for our sins and our forgiveness. Christ has risen from the grave so that you and I don't need any longer to fear the grave. In this saving work of Christ we are spiritually blessed beyond belief and measure.

But as this love of Christ has flowed *to* us, it doesn't always flow *through* us, into the hearts and lives of other people. People around us (like Lazarus around the rich man's table) are spiritually hungry and thirsty for the gospel message that only we can give. The plain question involves how the story of the cross and resurrection will ever come to anyone else if it doesn't flow through your lips and mine. Are we forcing the spiritually hungry Lazaruses around us to scrape for a few gospel crumbs, while the *feast* of the gospel message remains clogged in our own hearts?

We could start remedying this situation during our Sunday worship services. Let Christ flow through you when you worship with others. Let the hospitality of Christ you have in your heart flow through you to other worshipers as you greet one another before and after the service. Let the joy of Christ that you have in your heart flow through you in the songs and music, as you sing with enthusiasm — even loudly. Let the conviction of faith in Christ that you have in your heart flow through you as you speak the words of the Creed, not timidly, but firmly and in a spirit of testimony. So much of our public worship is lifeless because our faith is clogged within our hearts and needs to be freed up in vigorous expression and flow.

Equally importantly, you and I need to allow God's loving care and healing to flow through us, to others. Then we will refresh the lives of others, and our own lives will be constantly refreshed. That's what happened in Jesus' own life — all the way through his ministry. The Bible tells us that when Jesus began his ministry, he was filled with the Holy Spirit. That means that all of God's power and blessing were with Jesus, were in Jesus. Imagine if all of that divine power had gotten clogged within Jesus, if he would not have allowed that power that came to him to flow *through* him for the good and blessing of others.

But everywhere in his ministry we see God's power for good flowing through Christ. People were healed; people were brought to life; people received new hope for the future; people had their sins forgiven; storms were calmed and bread was multiplied — because Christ was not a bottleneck for God's saving power but was the very instrument through which God's blessings flowed to others. Jesus once observed that after a certain woman touched his robe, he felt the power of God going out from him to her. Jesus kept things flowing. God's power flowed through him to others.

Jesus never once faulted the man in the gospel story for being rich. That wasn't the point at all. The man's tragedy was that all his blessings got clogged. They never moved beyond his own heart or table. Blessings *to* him never became blessings *through* him. There was no recycling. To put it in biblical terms, the man wasn't practicing good stewardship. What was only loaned to him he thought he owned. He stopped the flow, the exhilaration, the fulfillment, the purpose, and the joy of life when he became a container instead of an instrument of God's blessings.

So in what area of life can you and I become instruments of God's loving care and healing? The answer is very simple: in those areas of life where we see human beings in need. Sometimes we see what we want to see and don't see what we don't want to see. But most of the time, I dare say, we see it all. It is just that in our sinful selfishness, we tell ourselves we cannot be bothered by the needs of other human beings. In the lengthy verses of this story that remain, Jesus makes it clear that if we have our minds and hearts made up not to hear and see, we probably won't. Jesus suggests the radical nature of the situation when he concludes here, "If they do not hear Moses and the prophets, neither will they be convinced if someone should rise from the dead" (v. 31).

But assuming that we have eyes that see, in what areas of life can we notice human beings in need? In every area. The situation in the text is dramatic and obvious. Lazarus, with his open sores and wretched appearance, was a high profile case of a person in need. The rich man should have known better; he should have noticed Lazarus.

Look around you in the places where you spend your day. You will notice people in need, I can assure you. Some of the people you work with have broken hearts and need ministry. People in your neighborhood are depressed and lonely, despite their cheerful greetings in passing. People in your church are going through crises as well as anyone else. Look around. You will see these people. They need a ministry that you could give. Let God's care for them flow through you.

In all of this maybe some of you are saying, "But that's not my cup of tea. Yes, I can give a buck to someone down and out, like Lazarus; but I don't know how to talk with people about their problems or help them." What you say could be true. But isn't there the possibility that you could learn some of the skills necessary in listening to other people and ministering to them? It is not unusual today for veteran workers in the marketplace to be expected to learn new skills as their jobs develop or expectations become altered. Within our churches today there are usually classes and courses offered for lay people who want to learn how to extend a ministry of caring to persons in need. Many medical and public agencies offer training for volunteers as well. Our friends and others need more than the crumbs of our quick smiles and a pat on the back. In this story Christ is talking about an in-depth ministry that needs to be done and should be done *now*.

God is blessing you richly each day. Don't become the place where God's blessings become clogged and stop. Keep things flowing. You will feel invigorated, and so will the persons who receive God's blessings *through* you.

Nobody Owes You Anything

Proper 22 *Luke 17:5-10*
Pentecost 20
Ordinary Time 27

This is the kind of sermon topic that the preacher hesitates to advertise ahead of time. If people come to church to hear some good news, this topic doesn't sound too promising. But I ask you to brace yourself and stick with it. The words we consider here are from the lips of none other than a merciful and loving Savior, the Lord Jesus Christ. His words often contained some hard truths, but they also finally reveal to us the marvelous, incredible goodness and love of God to you and me. So let's dare to tackle the topic, despite its unpromising sound — "Nobody Owes You Anything."

In a way, we know this is true. You and I ought to be grateful for everything we have; we ought to consider the whole sweep of our life as a gift that is given to us from the hand of providence. We owe our lives to God!

This is partly what the parable before us says. On the surface that's exactly what it seems to mean. Jesus portrays for us here a typical rural laborer of his day, perhaps a farmer coming in from plowing the fields all day, or a ranch hand who has been tending the sheep out on the range. In any case, Jesus calls this worker a servant, evidently one who was not part of the owner's family, and therefore one whom the owner had hired out of a gracious heart.

Now comes Jesus' key question. "Imagine you are that owner of the farm; when this hired servant of yours finishes his day and comes toward the farm yard, are you going to immediately invite him in to sit down at the table and eat?" The answer, Jesus would assume, is "no." He suggests that first of all you as the owner would sit down at the supper table and tell your worker to prepare a meal and serve it to you. Afterwards, even though it was a delicious meal, you would feel under no compulsion to gush over your servant and tell him what a good job he did. You can just get up and go to bed and let the servant eat the leftovers and then clean up. In fact, when you do leave the room, the hired hand ought to thank you for the privilege of serving you!

I think you would agree that the sermon topic succinctly expresses what Jesus wanted to say on the surface of this parable: nobody owes you anything. The world we live in is God's creation. In God's wisdom God has allowed us as God's creatures to inhabit the good world and enjoy its bounties. God has even given us as human beings an undeserved role of leadership in the world, it seems. But we are all stewards, so that if somehow we are getting along and making a living we ought to feel grateful and satisfied. If we are successful in the enterprise of life, we need to remember that we would be nothing without the nurturing that came from parents, from other relatives, from teachers and kind friends. Indeed, most of us only "get by with a little help from our friends." The whole universe, and our role in it, is a fantastic divine mystery for which we can take absolutely no credit; so every day ought to be Thanksgiving Day — a time to live in total gratitude to a host of forces outside ourselves. It's true: nobody owes you anything. In turn, you owe everything to God and others.

Beyond this obvious interpretation of the parable, perhaps Jesus also told it in a deeper sense — a parable to confront us with the spiritual truth about our eternal salvation. Again, Jesus would be saying that nobody *owes* us eternal life. The flip side is surely that you and I cannot claim or accomplish one single thing that would be considered a credit toward our salvation. We can work in the field all day long, all week long, for a lifetime, and there would still be no reason why God should feel indebted to save us. The comforting side — the gospel side — of what Jesus was saying in this parable would then be that God nevertheless *does* save us, evidently purely out of grace and love on God's part, since there is nothing we are bringing for credit.

It is easy to see that Jesus probably wanted his hearers to appreciate that side of the message in this parable, too. He wanted those listening to be impressed by the total humility that the servant in the parable exhibited. People are unworthy even to stand before God, much less to claim something of him. If they have done something that might possibly be interpreted in a positive way, it should be realized that they only did what was their duty. No claims can be connected with anything they have accomplished.

The Pharisees and other religious leaders, of course, were mostly the target of this parable. There didn't seem to be an inch of humility in any of them. If there were any club dues to pay, they considered themselves paid up. Like the Pharisee in another parable that Jesus told, these *Wunderkinder* of the religious world wouldn't grovel like the publican and pray, "God, be merciful to me, a sinner." They took care of their sins by themselves; they had a clean slate. There was no other payment needed. Nothing to do now but stand before God and accept the keys to heaven which God owed them.

As you can see, this parable becomes a way of proclaiming the Gospel in reverse. The parable unflinchingly claims that there is *nothing* we can do to merit our eternal salvation. The reverse side turns out to be that God therefore does *everything* for our salvation. The Good News is that in Jesus Christ God has done exactly that. Nobody owes us anything, but God goes ahead and does everything for our salvation anyway. When Christ mounts the cross, he is taking on his shoulder the debt of sin owed by the whole world. As the pain of crucifixion envelops him, he is embracing each one of us in the blood that cleanses us from all sin. Standing alive on Easter morning, he is providing a place for us to stand before the heavenly Father when we die. Standing there with other sinners, we'll be able to join hands and sing, "Nothing in my hand

I bring, simply to the cross I cling." God owes us nothing, but in that day Jesus will nevertheless say, "Come, O blessed of my Father, inherit the kingdom prepared for you ..." (Matthew 25:34).

But the final meaning of this parable lies even deeper than all of this. The deeper meaning comes to light when we go back to our theme sentence, "Nobody owes you anything." At the beginning of the sermon we said in effect that it would be presumptuous for anyone to deny that. Every rational person tends to assent to this truth. But then the final meaning of the parable — and its most challenging side, perhaps — pushes us not only to assent to such humility but also to live by that humility: to really practice the reality that nobody owes us anything! Put it this way: do we have the capacity to view one another in the same humble way that we now know we must view God? In other words, can you stand before *all other persons* and say, "I am an unworthy servant; I have only done what was my duty"?

What we do for God we should be willing to do for one another. *God* standing before us is our *neighbor* standing before us. Our neighbor standing before us is God standing before us. Jesus said all of this before, in another way, didn't he? " 'When did we see thee sick or in prison and visit thee?' And [God] will answer, '... as you did it to one of the least of these my brethren, you did it to me.' " (Matthew 25:39, 40). You see, the opposite of "Nobody owes you anything" is "You owe everybody everything!" Let self-righteous sinners like you and me try that one on for size. It is tough, tough, tough, because you and I so totally think, "Me, me, me." The fact is that when we probe and probe some more, you and I detest this proclamation, "Nobody owes you anything." And be sure of it, we detest this truth in regard to God also. There must be *something* God owes us! No, there isn't. There must be somebody in life I owe nothing to. No, there is not. There is never any other human being whom we can self-righteously pass by and say, "I owe you nothing!" Every last person, finally, is my neighbor. And when we serve that neighbor and are finished serving, we ought to say, "I am an unworthy servant; I have only done what was my duty." That is not false modesty; that is having the mind of Christ. That is *seeing* Christ in our neighbor.

Imagine how such a view would bring a new dignity to all other persons. But imagine how it would bring a new dignity to *you*, too! Now you are through and through a woman of Christ, a man of Christ. Your motives are (for once) totally clean. Love bathes your outlook. Self means nothing. God means everything. This is dignity, integrity. This is the way of Jesus Christ!

The great theologian Paul Tillich used to say, "Accept the fact that you're accepted." And we might add, "When you do, you will accept all others too and serve them. And no one will owe you anything." And you won't mind that at all.

In that other more famous parable, the one about the prodigal son, you will recall how Jesus spoke about a similar situation. After the heartwarming reunion of the younger son and his father, the older son comes in from laboring in the fields. He was one of those who appeared obedient and upright; his motives appeared impeccable; his devotion to his father seemed genuine. But when he is pressed to live out the total humility Jesus had in mind here, he breaks down. He cannot do it. He scorns his prodigal brother, and begins complaining at the top of his voice to his father. He blurts out claims about the father owing his brother nothing but owing him everything. Suddenly his long years of faithfulness appear ugly; his loyalty seems to have grown flat. He turns out to be the ungrateful son, in contrast to his younger brother who learned the lesson of gratefulness the hard way.

Whether we learn it from outward shame or inner bitterness, all of us need to be open to this shining godly humility. Today, as you stand bowed before the cross of the Savior, you will have at your disposal the power to claim the greatest gift any of us need: a grateful heart!

Lectionary Preaching After Pentecost

Virtually all pastors who make use of the sermons in this book will find their worship life and planning shaped by one of two lectionary series. Most mainline Protestant denominations, along with clergy of the Roman Catholic Church, have now approved — either for provisional or official use — the three-year Revised Common (Consensus) Lectionary. This family of denominations includes United Methodist, Presbyterian, United Church of Christ and Disciples of Christ. Recently the ELCA division of Lutheranism also began following the Revised Common Lectionary. This change has been reflected in the headings and scripture listings with each sermon in this book.

Roman Catholics and Lutheran divisions other than ELCA follow their own three-year cycle of texts. While there are divergences between the Revised Common and Roman Catholic/Lutheran systems, the gospel texts show striking parallels, with few text selections evidencing significant differences. Nearly all the gospel texts included in this book will, therefore, be applicable to worship and preaching planning for clergy following either lectionary.

A significant divergence does occur, however, in the method by which specific gospel texts are assigned to specific calendar days. The Revised Common and Roman Catholic Lectionaries accomplish this by counting backwards from Christ the King (Last Sunday after Pentecost), discarding "extra" texts from the front of the list: Lutherans (not using the Revised Common Lectionary) follow the opposite pattern, counting forward from The Holy Trinity, discarding "extra" texts at the end of the list.

The following index will aid the user of this book in matching the correct text to the correct Sunday during the Pentecost portion of the church year.

(Fixed dates do not pertain to Lutheran Lectionary)

Fixed Date Lectionaries *Revised Common (including ELCA)* *and Roman Catholic*	Lutheran Lectionary *Lutheran*
The Day of Pentecost	The Day of Pentecost
The Holy Trinity	The Holy Trinity
May 29-June 4 — Proper 4, Ordinary Time 9	Pentecost 2
June 5-11 — Proper 5, Ordinary Time 10	Pentecost 3
June 12-18 — Proper 6, Ordinary Time 11	Pentecost 4

June 19-25 — Proper 7, Ordinary Time 12	Pentecost 5
June 26-July 2 — Proper 8, Ordinary Time 13	Pentecost 6
July 3-9 — Proper 9, Ordinary Time 14	Pentecost 7
July 10-16 — Proper 10, Ordinary Time 15	Pentecost 8
July 17-23 — Proper 11, Ordinary Time 16	Pentecost 9
July 24-30 — Proper 12, Ordinary Time 17	Pentecost 10
July 31-Aug. 6 — Proper 13, Ordinary Time 18	Pentecost 11
Aug. 7-13 — Proper 14, Ordinary Time 19	Pentecost 12
Aug. 14-20 — Proper 15, Ordinary Time 20	Pentecost 13
Aug. 21-27 — Proper 16, Ordinary Time 21	Pentecost 14
Aug. 28-Sept. 3 — Proper 17, Ordinary Time 22	Pentecost 15
Sept. 4-10 — Proper 18, Ordinary Time 23	Pentecost 16
Sept. 11-17 — Proper 19, Ordinary Time 24	Pentecost 17
Sept. 18-24 — Proper 20, Ordinary Time 25	Pentecost 18
Sept. 25-Oct. 1 — Proper 21, Ordinary Time 26	Pentecost 19
Oct. 2-8 — Proper 22, Ordinary Time 27	Pentecost 20
Oct. 9-15 — Proper 23, Ordinary Time 28	Pentecost 21
Oct. 16-22 — Proper 24, Ordinary Time 29	Pentecost 22
Oct. 23-29 — Proper 25, Ordinary Time 30	Pentecost 23
Oct. 30-Nov. 5 — Proper 26, Ordinary Time 31	Pentecost 24
Nov. 6-12 — Proper 27, Ordinary Time 32	Pentecost 25
Nov. 13-19 — Proper 28, Ordinary Time 33	Pentecost 26 Pentecost 27
Nov. 20-26 — Christ the King	Christ the King

Reformation Day (or last Sunday in October) is October 31 (Revised Common, Lutheran)

All Saints' Day (or first Sunday in November) is November 1 (Revised Common, Lutheran, Roman Catholic)

Books In This Cycle C Series

Gospel Set

Sermons For Advent/Christmas/Epiphany
Deep Joy For A Shallow World
Richard A. Wing

Sermons For Lent/Easter
Taking The Risk Out Of Dying
Lee Griess

Sermons For Pentecost I
The Chain Of Command
Alexander H. Wales

Sermons For Pentecost II
All Stirred Up
Richard W. Patt

Sermons For Pentecost III
Good News Among The Rubble
J. Will Ormond

First Lesson Set

Sermons For Advent/Christmas/Epiphany
Where Is God In All This?
Tony Everett

Sermons For Lent/Easter
Returning To God
Douglas J. Deuel

Sermons For Pentecost I
How Long Will You Limp?
Carlyle Fielding Stewart, III

Sermons For Pentecost II
Lord, Send The Wind
James McLemore

Sermons For Pentecost III
Buying Swamp Land For God
Robert P. Hines, Jr.

www.ingramcontent.com/pod-product-compliance
Lightning Source LLC
Chambersburg PA
CBHW071731040426
42446CB00011B/2312